Heaven Can Wait,
Can Heaven Wait?

Heaven Can Wait,
Can Heaven Wait?

By
Agnes Ayo Akinola, RN.BS. MBA/ MHCM.PhD

Newburgh Press
Newburgh, Indiana
2018

Heaven Can Wait, Can Heaven Wait?

Newburgh Press
Newburgh, Indiana
2018

Table of Contents

An Abstract Of The Book
By: Agnes Akinola

Heaven Can Wait; Can Heaven Wait?

PURPOSE AND OBJECTIVE: To shed a new light into the Promise God made for us in (New International Version, John. 6. 51-58). As I bring the good news of our Lord to the sick and injured at bedside across and within my community of faith.

Jesus said to the Jewish crowds, "I am the Living bread that came down from heaven, whoever eats this bread will live forever; and the bread that I will give is my flesh for the life of the world." The Jews quarreled among themselves, saying, "How can this man give us his flesh to eat?" Jesus said to them, "Amen , amen, I say to you, unless you eat the flesh of the son of man and drink his blood, you do not have life within you. Whoever eats my flesh and drinks my blood has eternal life, and I will raise him on the last day. For my flesh is true food, and my blood is true drink. Whoever eats my flesh and drinks my blood remains in me and I in him, just as the living Father sent me and I have life because of the Father, so also the one who feeds on me will have life because of me. This is the bread that came down from heaven. Unlike your ancestors who ate and still died, whoever eats this bread will live forever." Jesus repeated this passage repeatedly so that we can get the true message of this heavenly peace, when someone repeated themselves over and over, we tend to take their words seriously, Jesus is never a joker, He came down for our salvation and throughout this essay, we will see the connection of heaven and how we the children of God ought to behave and claim our rightful heritage.

For many. Hell has become a fable, a myth an outdated story from the "Old Testament, a false doctrine according to some groups, which in actual fact a true Word of our God. There are so many false doctrine spreading throughout the universe right now, and the enemies want us to believe that there can be no such thing as eternal punishment for serious offense inflicted to another human being by another human beings while on earth, because in there mind, Jesus is God of Love and Kindness. Many have indeed throw Hell and punishment out of the gospel and preach prosperity along with concern for sin.

Their rationale, if there is no Hell, and then there can be no concern for sin. But let's see what Malachi said (New International Version Malachi 3.6). "I am the Lord and I change not". So our enemies want us to lower our guard and do as we pleased, but I say be careful Christians, because we have no idea when the owner of the vineyard will come. And If He does come we hope He finds us with good work. So, Faith without work is dead.

Remember by their free will and choice they rejected God while on earth and thus excluded themselves from communion with Him and are damned forever. (Douay-Rheims American, Sirach. 21.10). "The congregation of sinners is like tow heaped together, and the end of them is a flame of fire". Heavenly promise in (NIV, Revelation. 21. 1-5). "Then I saw a new heaven and a new earth, for the first heaven and the first earth had passed away, and the sea was no more. And I saw the holy city, New Jerusalem, coming down out of heaven from God, prepared as a bride adorned for her husband. And I heard a loud voice from the throne saying, "Behold, the dwelling place of God is with man.

He will dwell with them, and they will be his people, and God Himself will be with them as their God. He will wipe away every tear from their eyes, and death shall be no more, neither shall there be mourning, nor crying, nor pain anymore, for the former things have passed away". And He who was seated on the throne said, "Behold,

Iam making all things new." Also, He said, "Write this down, for these words are true".

The story of Jesus offers a new hope for humanity and confronts each individual with a personal touch. The story, one can conclude starts with God being already on the stage by Himself. He created the universe by Himself and thus allowed the human race to share His glory and splendor. See what the Lord said in (New American Standard Bible Isaiah 55.10-11). And (NASB, Psalms. 8. 1-9).

10. "For as the rain and the snow come down from heaven,

And do not return there without watering the earth

And making it bear and sprout,

And furnishing seed to the sower and bread to the eater;

11. So will My word be which goes forth from My mouth;

It will not return to Me empty,

Without accomplishing what I desire,

And without succeeding in the matter for which I sent".

We have to find ourselves in the story of our God. We must obey His word and commandments to better prepare ourselves for the sacred Journey each and every one of us face. In (NIV, Deuteronomy, 6.5-7). This Bible passage, Moses reminded the Israelites the Ten Commandments, and again in Deuteronomy 5.32-33). He instructed them to "Love the Lord thy God" and remember His saving grace. Our God is Supreme Being, who is His own existence and is infinitely perfect. He accomplishes all things, in Him nothing is impossible. He sees things and knows all things, whatever we all are going through. He is omnipotent, Omnipresent, Omniscience. (NASB, Psalms. 139. 1-24.)

He will judge the "Living and the Dead", He's just and fair God. We should never delegate our own "Eternity" to anybody. We should as individual work at it with our giving talent, spiritually, body and soul.

We all are going on the journey and none of us is even prepared, until some of us take ill and in the hospital, when we get there, we can't figure things out, we get frustrated because for the first time, perhaps some of us never depended on others to help them before, now here we are, in the hospital with bunch of strangers.

In any given U.S hospitals the settings take the shape or form of " United Nation" staring at you, and if you are not a social or have not interacted with adults both publicly and privately for a long time, this could pose a problem for you, this is as candid as it can get as Christian to another Christian, you're about to freak out, even your assigned doctor have accents, you have accents, then the second commandment smiles at you which means "JESUS" Love your neighbor as yourself.

You meet these people outside your comfort zone, away from families and friends, you ask yourself what's happening to me, you think your world is falling apart or you're falling apart, but you're not, it's just that you're trying to make sense of this situation, but you can't or guess what? why you're trying to figure things out, your nurse came in, she introduced herself, she's from India, your aide came in she's from Caribbean Island, your doctor came in she's from Mideast, and his assistant (female) is from Asia, and your x-ray lady came in she's from Mexico, your chaplain came in she's from Africa, and lastly your pharmacist came in he's an American, then you asks yourself I'm still in America? but you forgot the story of" Tower of Babel" in the Bible. The Israelites thought they were home free now, because they survived the storm? Ha Ha

These are Americans, fellow citizens like you, oh you lied to your nurse you're not in any psychotropic drug, now you're shaking like a leaf because you did not remember to take you medicine this morning , as part of your drug screening for admission your blood level just confirmed you were on anti-depressant drug, and the nurse knew, so you panicked due to serious nature of the illness or denial of your prognosis and outcome, instead of you praying to One and only God who can make you well and better, you bargaining with God. Lord if you let me live this time I promise I'd be good.

I will turn from my bad self; adopt behavior worthy of Almighty Father, as if we can buy God. We equate God's Love with commodities and things of interest we buy each other's as   gifts, money or other things we give for affection.

Our Lord did not need anything from us, all He ever wanted from us, is to show some Love, Respect and Humility that we appreciate Him and we Love Him back.

When people are sick, the individual persons are now separated from their home churches, the pastors or Clergy's can't leave the flocks and attend to you one on one, but some hospitals are good enough to add and accommodate the Spiritual model of spiritual heritage and care for those who are sick among us through donation from public and volunteering department .

None of us knows the time when He will come back again, He did not even reveal His coming and judgment day to His Holy Angels, but He told us to be vigilant and pray without season, so that even if He come He will find good work with us, we don't even have to go nowhere, look around us and each other, we live in a world where everything is Me, Me, and Me. No room for others in our lives. Charity begins at home, in our neighborhood, public and private schools. churches, senior centers across this nation, volunteering those gifts of time for each other.

I deal each day with sick people, wonderful people young and old, some of them will go back home after this illness, and some will never go back home forever depending on the nature of their sickness and their age, only God can call individual home.

I am a nurse by profession and a pastoral care hospital minster. My work as a hospital care minister is   an extension of my role as a profession nurse this is how God Almighty intended it; He is the keeper of "Time".

A beautiful Christian heritage was handed down to us many years ago, yet many of us still don't know or how to use the gifts. We have to own it and pass the teachings and doctrine of Jesus Christ along the path of new generation of Christians. Our God is God of order and Holiness, and by His blood we were" healed".

We have to come back to Him; we must take up our own crosses and follow Jesus. Here is what Deuteronomy said in NIV 6. 5-7. "You shall love the Lord with all your heart and with all your soul and might. And these words that I command you today shall be on your heart. You shall teach them diligently to your children and shall talk of them when you sit in your house, and when you walk by the way, and when you lie down, and when you rise."

Throughout the journey of faith, God has always come for His people, which is why now than ever to trust in His goodness and rest assure He will get us home to "Paradise" For us joy and happiness is found along the way and not at the end of the road, meaning as we try to unlock the chain of Sin and exit the valley of death, we pray God provide us with all available resources to conquer the enemies of our salvation.

Again in (English Standard Version, Proverbs 3. 5-6). illustrated yet another point, trusting in the Lord, having an assurance that if God Says Trust me, it meant Trust in the Lord. "Trust in the Lord with all your heart and lean not on your own understanding, in all your ways acknowledges Him and He will make your paths straight."

The question then is "Heaven can wait: Can Heaven wait? The Four Last Things is real. The judgement, Heaven, Hell and Eternal punishment. Which side are you on?

Here are some of the question people online are asking? If God is a God of Love, how could He condemn anyone to eternal punishment?' The argument will just blow your minds; this is how some people on online responded to some of the question posted by some Christian's bloggers

Many people justified their sinful lifestyle with ignorance and the attitude of entitlement. In their minds, Jesus will not do anything to them because they believe He existed and that as long as they stay away from these sins and that sins they will not go to hell, indeed none of us knows how our Lord judges or who for that matter will end up with the Lord on that day, but as children of God Most High we are call to admonish things that do not either make sense or lack moral aptitude, or for that matter lack christains virtues. The answer is simple, God is God of righteousness and justice, our Lord is not Santa Clause which comes out every Christmas dishes out gifts to people on their good behavior. His justice demands eternal punishment for those who do not live according to the righteous laws that reflect His nature (Scott 150). Let's put this in a perspective and not kid ourselves, (NKJV, Ezekiel.18.20-32.). Jesus came to fulfil the laws not to abolish them.

The good news is that by believing in His Son Jesus Christ who took away the sins of the world, the price had been paid on our behalf. Therefore, brothers and sisters believe in our Lord Jesus, renounce sins and pick up your crosses today and follow the REAL JESUS.

My Project is a Persuasive, Retreat and Revival with family unity/connectedness as you go through, you will encounter Jesus and find yourself in the story of God. You will tour with me, the story of" Tower of Babel", "The Samaritan woman", the story of Ruth and Naomi", "The creation story", and yes our Lord birth announcement" Nicodemus question on repentance and being born again. Our Lord personal story and frustration about our uncaring attitudes, and His death and the legacy He left behind". His story is our story. We serve the Living God. Again, you will go with me to the hospital as a pastoral minister and as a nurse with dying patients; my project is bi-vocational in nature.

Acknowledgement and Thank You.

I would like to thank the following people, my husband, my children, my deceased mother, my deceased senior brother, deceased sister Betty. Lynn Liebengood at my school, she never interrupted me once during my calling to the school, she allowed me to vent my frustrations, fears and emotions and she will gently say "How can I help?" To Dr. Glenn Mollette, my professor and president of my school, who followed and yielded to God's Calling – Ambassador for Christ. And thanks to the many professors that I did not get a chance to meet due to my online classes and long distance education. My love to you all. To Father Page who coordinated my admission process into The Catholic Chaplain Corps for the Archdiocese of Galveston-Houston in the Pastoral Assistants Formation/training 2012. To Father Peter at Corpus Christi Church in Houston who trained me how to be a good listener at bedside during hospital visit. Father Bob and deceased father Dana who forwarded my recommendation letter to the Corps. To father Anthony, Fr. Chris Alimaji who forwarded my recommendation letter to St. Mary Seminary for my Pastoral Care Ministers training 2015. To Ms. Denice Foose who recommended me from Baylor St. Luke's Medical Center-Mission and Spiritual Care Department and Clinical Pastoral Education Department. To my deceased best friend Tippy Stuart, a devoted mother, grandma and champion of volunteerism. To Mary, my preceptor, in 2013 who met me where I was and encouraged me to be myself on my first day at St. Luke's Medical Center in Houston as pastoral assistant in the department of Spiritual care/chaplaincy. I was so nervous that day, she saw through me but passed no judgement, after four weeks, she wrote a beautiful recommendation to Father Peter that "Agnes is good to go" meaning I could function "Solo" without a doubt in her mind. To Mrs. Beatrice Cunningham my Bible Study Class Coordinator at St. Philip Neri. To my prayer warriors my sisters in the Lord at Sisters of St. Clare in Saginaw, Michigan who always pray for me at prayer request sessions/petitions each day. Finally, to all the wonderful people I met at St. Luke's my fellow Pastoral Assistants, Chaplains and Pastoral Care Ministers. To all our faithful departed friends and relatives, may their souls rest in peace of our Lord. Amen.

CHAPTER 1.
Introduction

1.1 Journey of Faith

The descendants of Abraham were given the tasks to evangelized and bring children of our Lord from different nationalities to our Lord's Table. John the Baptist pointed out the Lamb for us, Peter the Rock firmly established His Throne, and Apostle Paul prepared the Bride for us in one Triune God. The churches keep the alliance moving forward, and we experienced this through each other's, whether in our Sunday gathering, weekdays Bible study groups or volunteering our gifts of time in various ministries within the Body of Christ (Church).

Our Lord spirit always guide and power us to move forward with His divine calling in each and every one of us is evident in our ways and deeds, the fact that our diversity and cultural differences make us unique and we all see the work of God in all of us should make us happy.

Our foundation must be on the "Rock "Jesus solid ground (Luke 6:48 NIV) ... Stress is a form of fear which can trickle down to lack of faith, Greed is the fear of poverty, which could impede our success with lack of giving, the second Commandment which the Lord said love your neighbor as yourself, by not giving through the charities out there for the needy and the poor we stop God blessing into our lives. And to focus solely on work and acquisition of wealth without praising and using the money for things necessary for God that is a sin, remembered a question came to Jesus while He was preaching, it was money issue, our Lord asked the people who posed the question at me,

He said whose head was marked on the coin, the people said Caesar, then our Lord replied them "Give to Caesar things that are Caesar, and to God things that are God" immediately the people left His sight. See when we help our brothers and sisters in charities whatever we give are safe with the Lord, fear, selfishness, pride, and indifference, all these things opposed God character. This Tug-of-war surface because we are wrestling with our own flesh, we put Christ in second place, instead of putting Him first. How then can we please God and do the will of God, by believing His word and do the will of the Father, the Bible passage (New International Version, Matthew. 16.25-27). helped us to eye ball the promise and those with faith got the message. This message was said by Jesus right after Peter declared Him a Messiah when He answered Jesus Christ was the Son of Living God and our Messiah. 25 For whoever wants to save their life[a] will lose it, but whoever loses their life for me will find it. 26 What good will it be for someone to gain the whole world, yet forfeit their soul? Or what can anyone give in exchange for their soul? 27 For the Son of Man is going to come in his Father's glory with his angels, and then he will reward each person according to what they have done.

Footnotes:
a. Matthew 16:25 The Greek word means either life or soul; also in verse 26.

1.2 The Divine Plan

Have we ever asked ourselves this question, Why I am here? Are we here just to watch others passing us by, or are we here just to be here and occupy space.

Is God Almighty who brought us here just want us to be here without accomplishing anything, and knowing that while He Himself was on Earth, left no stone untouched and said on the last message to God the Father when He was praying for us that , all the God The Father had given Him, He had shared everything with us, and that now   He's going to Heaven prayed nothing should happened to us, and that He will provide Holy Spirit "The Comforter to be with us to keep us safe' .

If our Lord knew the harshness and the wickedness out in the world, and shared those thoughts with us through prayers, how come we the children of God can't do it, we just have to ask ourselves these candid questions

1. Why did He come down to Earth?
2. Why did He Himself pick a family?
3. Why did He pick this tribe-The Israelites?
4. What really is God mission on Earth?

We are not here by chance, on the contrary, many science fictions tried to tell the story of God for sensationalized thrills by what He did and created, and we worship our creation rather than giving Him the respect due Him. Francis Collins a notable scientist wrote, "The universe had a beginning, that it obeys orderly laws that can be expressed precisely with mathematics and the existence of a remarkable series of "Coincidences" that allow the laws of nature to support life, what kind of God must be behind it, what kind of intelligence and what kind of mind? (Collins 219). So, ponder on the above statement for a minute. Then Thank the Lord for your own life.

When we see ourselves, we see Our God in His Holy Trinity. The Father, the Son and Holy Spirit. We can't separate these three (Three in One). The Holy Trinity is our heart beat, our food, and our life.

So, let's follow the story of our Lord, and at the end of this story journey, we will find that, 1. God exist. 2. God will continue to exist. 3. We will know that He loved us so much and does not want harm to fall on us. 4. Heaven our Lord home can't wait? And we belong there that was His intension in the first place to be with Him in Heaven after the journey here on Earth ends, as long we have not told Him to "hands-off".

We must get it, the moment He created us, He had place His Seal in each and everyone us His angels to lead us back to Him in His Kingdom of Heaven, we all leave temporarily here on earth just like He did once, and we all will leave forever with Him provided we have not cancel Him out of our lives.

In our daily journey, we need Him, Faith of our fathers and mothers. Holy Faith. Jesus already knows which church you and I go to and none, trust me if you're not aware of that yourself. No need to play the church card with the Lord or ridicule some people that do not belong to your denominations. The most important question to ask is, the church you and I affiliate ourselves with, we pray for Jesus sake are truthful to the gospel of Jesus and His teachings, and we will join Him when this journey here on earth ends? Amen.

We came with nothing and we leave with nothing, if you don't believe me come with me and I will let you tour my town and go to morgue with me, as a nurse for twenty-five years, patients have died in front of me/or in my arms. I have performed many post mortem care before families come in to say their byes, removed all life sustaining equipment from the body, et cetera.

I have called county morgue to pick-up remains of citizens due to social economic status or simply deceased persons had no relationship with families who are still alive and they refused to call back the hospital, this cut across social economic boundaries, at the same time I have seen other beautiful families with courage and decency who provided nurses and doctors the funeral homes to take their loved ones even though they have no idea patients were ill or living nearby. Please as you go through this writing, note that the ministry of pastoral care of the sick is one of the many ministries belong to our God, we are one together a big family in the Kingdom of our Lord. (NIV, Ephesians.2.1-10.) And (NIV, I Corinthians. 12.3-11.).

1.3 The Story of God the Creation of the World
(NIV, Genesis. 1.1-31)

1. In the beginning, God created the heavens and the earth.

2. The earth was without form and void, and darkness was over the face of the deep. And the Spirit of God was hovering over the face of the waters.

3. And God said, let there be light," and there was light.

4. And God saw that the light was good. And God separated the light from the darkness.

5. God called the light Day, and the darkness he called Night. And there was evening and there was morning, the first day.

6. And God said, "Let there be an expanse1 in the midst of the waters, and let it separate the waters from the waters."

7. And God made2 the expanse and separated the waters that were under the expanse from the waters that were above the expanse. And it was so. 8 And God called the expanse Heaven.3 And there was evening and there was morning, the second day.

9. And God said, "Let the waters under the heavens be gathered together into one place, and let the dry land appear." And it was so.

10. God called the dry land Earth, and the waters that were gathered together he called Seas. And God saw that it was good.

11. And God said, "Let the earth sprout vegetation, plants5 yielding seed, and fruit trees bearing fruit in which is their seed, each according to its kind, on the earth." And it was so.

12. The earth brought forth vegetation, plants yielding seed according to their own kinds, and trees bearing fruit in which is their seed, each according to its kind. And God saw that it was good.

13. And there was evening and there was morning, the third day.

14. And God said, "Let there be lights in the expanse of the heavens to separate the day from the night. And let them be for signs and for seasons, and for days and years,

15. and let them be lights in the expanse of the heavens to give light upon the earth." And it was so.

16. And God made the two great lights—the greater light to rule the day and the lesser light to rule the night—and the stars.

17. And God set them in the expanse of the heavens to give light on the earth,

18. to lure over the day and over the night, and to separate the light from the darkness. And God saw that it was good.

19. And there was evening and there was morning, the fourth day.

20. And God said, "Let the waters swarm with swarms of living creatures, and let birds fly above the earth across the expanse of the heavens."

21. So God created the great sea creatures and every living creature that moves, with which the waters swarm, according to their kinds, and every winged bird according to its kind. And God saw that it was good.

22. And God blessed them, saying, "Be fruitful and multiply and fill the waters in the seas, and let birds multiply on the earth."

23. And there was evening and there was morning, the fifth day.

24. And God said, "Let the earth bring forth living creatures according to their kinds—livestock and creeping things and beasts of the earth according to their kinds." And it was so. 25 And God made the beasts of the earth according to their kinds and the livestock according to their kinds, and everything that creeps on the ground according to its kind. And God saw that it was good.

26. Then God said, "Let us make man in our image, after our likeness. And let them have dominion over the fish of the sea and over the birds of the heavens and over the livestock and over all the earth and over every creeping thing that creeps on the earth."

27. So God created man in his own image, In the image of God, he created him; Male and female he created them.

28. And God blessed them. And God said to them, s"Be fruitful and

multiply and fill the earth and subdue it, and have dominion over the fish of the sea and over the birds of the heavens and over every living thing that moves on the earth."

29. And God said, "Behold, I have given you every plant yielding seed that is on the face of all the earth, and every tree with seed in its fruit. You shall have them for food.

30. "And to every beast of the earth and to every bird of the heavens and to everything that creeps on the earth, everything that has the breath of life, I have given every green plant for food." And it was so.

31. "And with everything that he had made, and behold, it was very good. And there was evening and there was morning, the sixth day.

1.4 The Creation of man and woman

2 Thus the heavens and the earth were completed, and all their hosts.2 By the seventh day God completed His work which He had done, and He rested on the seventh day from all His work which He had done.3 Then God blessed the seventh day and sanctified it, because in it He rested from all His work which God had created [a] and made.

4 This is the account of the heavens and the earth when they were created, in the day that the Lord God made earth and heaven. 5 Now no shrub of the field was yet in the earth, and no plant of the field had yet sprouted, for the Lord God had not sent rain upon the earth, and there was no man to [b]cultivate the ground. 6 But a [c] mist used to rise from the earth and water the whole surface of the ground. 7 Then the Lord God formed man of dust from the ground and breathed into his nostrils the breath of life; and man became a living being. 8 The Lord God planted a garden toward the east, in Eden; and there He placed the man whom He had formed. 9 Out of the ground the Lord God caused to grow every tree that is pleasing to the sight and good

for food; the tree of life also in the midst of the garden, and the tree of the knowledge of good and evil.

10 Now a river] flowed out of Eden to water the garden; and from there it divided and became four rivers. 11 The name of the first is Pishon; it flows around the whole land of Havilah, where there is gold.

12. The gold of that land is good; the bdellium and the onyx stone are there.

13. The name of the second river is Gihon; it flows around the whole land of Cush.

14. The name of the third river is Tigris; it [1]flows east of Assyria. And the fourth river is the Euphrates.

15 Then the Lord God took the man and put him into the Garden of Eden to cultivate it and keep it.

16. The Lord God commanded the man, saying, "From any tree of the garden you may eat freely;

17. but from the tree of the knowledge of good and evil you shall not eat, for in the day that you eat from it you will surely die."

18. Then the Lord God said, "It is not good for the man to be alone; I will make him a helper suitable for him."

19. Out of the ground the Lord God formed every beast of the field and every bird of the sky, and brought them to the man to see what he would call them; and whatever the man called a living creature, that was its name.

20. The man gave names to all the cattle, and to the birds of the sky, and to every beast of the field, but for [r]Adam there was not found a helper]suitable for him.

21. So the Lord God caused a deep sleep to fall upon the man, and he slept; then He took one of his ribs and closed up the flesh at that place.

22. The Lord God fashioned into a woman the rib which He had taken from the man, and brought her to the man.

23. The man said,

"This is now bone of my bones,

And flesh of my flesh;

She shall be called Woman,

Because [w]she was taken out of Man."

24. For this reason a man shall leave his father and his mother and be joined to his wife; and they shall become one flesh. 25 And the man and his wife were both naked and were not ashamed.

1.5 The Discussion the Tree of the Knowledge of Good and Evil

After God perfectly sets the above stage for Adam and Eve and literally gives them everything under the sun, He told them that there was one thing they cannot do. He told them not to eat from the tree of knowledge of good and evil, they can eat the rest in the garden, but our forefather disobeyed God and went and ate from the tree, they confessed and told Him what happened and who told them to eat apples, the enemy of God is our enemy and our enemies are God enemy due to our Divinely Covenant with Almighty Father. For disobeying God our Forefather Adam and Eve were punished, so was the enemy who made them to fall, but the deed had already done, it would take another Covenant from our God to rectify the damage, so God called Abraham for the task. The more we get it, the better for us so that we can better equip ourselves and ask God for assistance. We are their descendants, and Jesus came to pay that price, because the wages of sin is death, but His true gift to us is eternal salvation. In (NIV, Genesis 1.29-31 Genesis 2.1-3 NIV). Our God was pleased with His accomplishment. He had hope we love He just like He had loved us, but instead we were never satisfied. We hurt one another in our quest to store up riches and wealth, knowing that none of us we take them with us after this journey ends, yet we scorned Him and neglected our Christians value. I hope the readers find Jesus Story worth exploring and decide to follow our Lord with their crosses, Amen.

1.6 Worship of Creation rather than Creator
(NASB, Wisdom. 13.1-19)

We pay attention to toys more than our God, which is why He warn us to be careful and not let the creation of things overwhelm us and forget the owner of the universal, because one day, we might have to account for our life's journey. "What shall it profit a man, if he gains the whole world and loose his soul"? We have to put things in perspective. Tension arose when our "Fore parent" separated from God and seek their own counsel.

They listened to the deceptive voice of the enemy and doubt God's trustworthiness. Since then none of our lives have been the same, the curse will forever be there, the sin has been committed and it will take another covenant to set it right...

The creator banished Adam and Eve from the "Garden". Garden of Eden will forever be a place of refuge in God the father and will take another person-the second person of the Holy Trinity to bridge the divide and reconciled us back to God.

Lack of judgement and disobedience could steal our joy away from us; we have to be careful with whom we associate ourselves with. A once home to Adam and Eve is now unreachable, the garden is now a fortified Garden with Angels all around guarding the place 24 hours/ seven. Have you noticed, we compete so much now with different entity in the universal, but God is always on our side, He will make a way when there are no way, because His Mercy endured forever. We will get back to "Garden of Eden" if we listen to Jesus and follow His Divine path as He had laid down for us. Remember our sins separate us from God.

b. Digression on False Worship.

Have you noticed we have become Nature Worship?

1. Foolish by nature were all who were in ignorance of God, And who from the good things seen did not succeed in knowing the one who is,*And from studying the works did not discern the artisan; a

2. Instead either fire, or wind, or the swift air,
Or the circuit of the stars, or the mighty water,
Or the luminaries of heaven, the governors* of the world, they considered gods'

3. Now if out of joy in their beauty they thought them gods,
Let them know how far more excellent the Lord is than these; For the original source of beauty fashioned them

4. Or if they were struck by their might and energy, Let them realize from these things how much more powerful is the one who made them.

5. For from the greatness and the beauty of created things
Their original author, by analogy, is seen.

6. But yet, for these the blame is less;*
For they have gone astray perhaps,
Though they seek God and wish to find him.

7. For they search busily among his works,
But are distracted by what they see, because the things seen are fair.

8. But again, not even these are pardonable.

9. For if they so far succeeded in knowledge
That they could speculate about the world,
How did they not more quickly find its Lord?

c . Idolatry

10. But wretched are they, and in dead things are their hopes,
Who termed gods things made by human hands:

Gold and silver, the product of art, and images of beasts, or useless stone, the work of an ancient hand.

d. The Carpenter and Wooden idols.

11. A carpenter may cut down a suitable tree and skillfully scrape off all its bark, And deftly plying his art produce something fit for daily use,

12. And use the scraps from his handiwork in preparing his food, and have his fill;

13. Then the good-for-nothing refuse from these remnants, crooked wood grown full of knots, he takes and carves to occupy his spare time This wood he models with mindless skill, and patterns it on the image of a human being

14. or makes it resemble some worthless beast. When he has daubed it with red and crimsoned its surface with red stain, and daubed over every blemish in it,

15. He makes a fitting shrine for it and puts it on the wall, fastening it with a nail.

16. Thus he provides for it lest it fall down, knowing that it cannot help itself; for, truly, it is an image and needs help

17. But when he prays about his goods or marriage or children he is not ashamed to address the thing without a soul. For vigor he invokes the powerless;

18. for life he entreats the dead; For aid he beseeches the wholly incompetent; for travel, something that cannot even walk;

19. For profit in business and success with his hands

The Lord God Will Seek Them Out for the lost children of our God, even though they run but they will not run away forever due to the saving graceof our Lord. (ESV, Ezekiel. 34. 11-16).

11. "For thus says the Lord God: Behold, I, I myself will search for my sheep and will seek them out. 12 As a shepherd seeks out his flock

when he is among his sheep that have been scattered, so will I seek out my sheep, and I will rescue them from all places where they have been scattered on a day of clouds and thick darkness. 13 And I will bring them out from the peoples and gather them from the countries and will bring them into their own land. And I will feed them on the mountains of Israel, by the ravines, and in all the inhabited places of the country. 14 I will feed them with good pasture, and on the mountain heights of Israel shall be their grazing land. There they shall lie down in good grazing land, and on rich pasture they shall feed on the mountains of Israel. 15 I myself will be the shepherd of my sheep, and I myself will make them lie down, declares the Lord God. 16 I will seek the lost, and I will bring back the strayed, and I will bind up the injured, and I will strengthen the weak, and the fat and the strong I will destroy.[a] I will feed them in justice.

Footnotes:

a. Ezekiel 34:16 Vulgate I will watch over

CHAPTER 2:
Methodology of Lectio Divina
the Empowerment Tool

2.1 "Lectio" Divina Reading

Lectio Divina: is a method for praying with the scripture. It had been in practice for many years since the mediaeval time as the monks prepared their Liturgy of hour. St. Augustine of Hippo phrase it "Ever ancient ever new", it described the newly interest many churches around the world are using in their Bible study programs or weekly Bible study gatherings, it is an effective way of reading, meditating and comprehending what is read.

You may ask, why do we focus on the way we read the sacred Text, because the Sacred Text is our daily bread, everything we do in life as Christians revolve around the Bible.

Our Lord's preaching, teachings, His healing ministry, all the parables to make our lives better are recorded in the Sacred Text. Whenever He wants to talk to us, He either refers to a passage or gives us an inspirational guidance on what to do. So, reading and praying with scripture is the method I will use to carry this report to my audiences in this persuasive report, to follow the plan God Almighty has mapped out for us.

From Genesis to Revelation as we read, we will encounter our Lord words and actions, the sacred scripture is a "Living Ledger/Text", where we go every day to receive blessings from above. Our world is not a perfect world. He told us to believe and trust His words, we must pray with scripture to have knowledge of our God, for all our undertakings and for others in our lives.

2.2. The method of Lectio Divina follows four basis steps:

My goal is to simplify a way whereby lay Christians could read and understand the passage he/she just read without complication or confusion, and that individual can turn around and share in his/her own words with the group, this is empowerment and joy with our gifts of time with each other. We will refer to chapter two for our Bible passages to connect with audiences back and forth, thus chapter two is our "Bible Passages Hub".

A. Step One Lectio or   Reading

No rush, pace yourself, approach, read a short chapter instead of a large section of scripture, or you can break your passages into sequence to prevent sensory overload, tiredness, or boredom.

B. Step two Meditatio - Meditation

Reflection on what is read, think over what you just read; allow the mind to settle, and to connect with your/mine heart.

C. Step Three Contemplatio -Contemplation

Open your heart to receive the word let God in, pray within your heart. Allow God's grace to come in to reactivate His blessings on you.

D. Step Four. Oratio prayer

Take your time to talk with God, do not rush, invite God into your heart, and let Him do the talking for you, allow the prompting of the Holy Spirit, relax and listen to God talking with you.

Reading a Bible is a special time for any Christian, we know the moment we open the Bible we are going to encounter our Lord Jesus in the passage we venerated in front of ourselves whether today's reading is in Old Testament or New Testament, His word is everlasting.

Many churches around the world, lectio Divina provides a simple but prayerful method for faith sharing, each participant share the word of God, not just one person reading and preaching, teaching, no monopoly of time and effort, each member participate equally for effective meeting. We validate each other with our gift of time, let's face it, on that day, we will all be alone to face Jesus at the judgment seat of God, what a way to prepare and know the scripture for ourselves, what I'm trying to say, for us knowing basic scripture reading with comprehension ,and the ability to recall it when we are call upon or in any christains gathering is positive for us, because if our foundation is good, and we believe in Jesus Christ, nothing can shake a good foundation.

We must warn one another of the consequences of sin and have awareness and challenges. Let see what Jesus said about good foundation. Are we like foolish person, who built his/her house on sand, or are we like wise person who built his/her house on solid ground with words of Jesus Christ? This story is from (ESV, Matthew 7.24-27).

24 "Everyone then who hears these words of mine and does them will be like a wise man who built his house on the rock. 25 And the rain fell, and the floods came, and the winds blew and beat on that house, but it did not fall, because it had been founded on the rock. 26 And everyone who hears these words of mine and does not do them will be like a foolish man who built his house on the sand. 27 And the rain fell, and the floods came, and the winds blew and beat against that house, and it fell, and great was the fall of it."

The above passage came straight from our Lord' mouth, we have to take and believe every word He told us. He told us to trust Him and be safe. So, for this project, the question we need to ask ourselves will be, Heaven can wait; Can Heaven wait? Heaven is our last quest, are we really prepared for it, or are we just winking or faking it, praying it will never come. He created the Heaven and Hell. Two groups-one will enter His gate, and other group will select the later due to our disobedience on our part and uncaring attitude to self and others.

I hope my audiences enjoy the project/Essay. (NIV, John. 3-16). "For God so loved the world, that He gave His beloved Son, that whosoever believe in Him, should not perish, but have everlasting life." Again, another perspective (NASB, Act. 1. 10-12). 10 And as they were gazing intently into the sky while He was going, behold, two men in white clothing stood beside them. 11 They also said, "Men of Galilee, why do you stand looking into the sky? This Jesus, who has been taken up from you into heaven, will come in just the same way as you have watched Him go into Heaven. Then my question to anyone out there is "Heaven can wait; Can Heaven Wait? We must read the Bible to get us prepare for the four last things. We owe that to Jesus Christ, the author of our faith and finisher of our lives.

Footnotes:
a. Matthew 7:25
b. John 3:16
c. Act 1: 10

2.3 Meditation Guide

For this persuasive report, I will use New American Standard Bible in my meditation technique. Individual can use their favorite translation of the Bible.

We will put on the lens of diversity and inclusion as we use the following steps, which are an adaptation of the Lectio Divina process of meditating and praying with scripture, for the explanation and process of Lectio Divina for more clarity please go back to chapter two; section one in which it was explained fully. We fail if we disobey His commandments. Let us leave everything to Jesus, He Cares for us.

As with any job interview, individual going for a job interview does his/her homework prior to the event, we know a whole lot of the company or organization we are doing the interview with, how long the business we want to be part of has been in existent, the pay rate or starting pay grade, the company benefit, how strong the business within the community, etc., and for the big day, we are well prepare and we answer all question to the best of our ability, in fact, due to desperation how much we need the job, we out performed, so if we can work hard to get a job and be out again before the ninety days up, why can't we take the homework of our Lord seriously,

He invited us to come dine with Him, and before He left, He broke bread and wine with His twelve Apostles, and they passed down the ritual to us for remembrance of His Mercy. And in all Christians gathering each Sundays, or monthly we proclaim His death and His resurrection, yet some Christians have no clue His coming back again, or what we need to do before He comes.

1. Pray a prayer to the Holy Spirit, then ask Jesus to be with you to give you insights, thoughts and actions that will help you increase your appreciation of diversity and become more inclusive in every area of your life.

2. Read the scripture of the day silently. Pay attention to the word, phrase or sentence that strike you (pause 5 minutes or more) Meditate, think what and why? then write in your prayer journal. (check the back of this report for journaling).

3. Read the scripture aloud. There will be a word, phrase or sentence that strike you, Ponder, and think about them and write what your thoughts are in your prayer journal.

4. Read the same scripture aloud again, if you are doing this with your group, use another person to read the scripture aloud the second time. After listening to the readings take time to meditate, ponder on the words and ask Jesus. "What are you saying to me about diversity and inclusion in this scripture passage? Write down your thoughts. (pause 10 minutes *).

5. Take the time to pray with scripture, meditate with Jesus about any situation or thoughts that come to mind. You may want to ask for help. Praise God or thank God. You may include your prayers in your journal. (pause for 5 minutes).

6. Read over the comments you have written. Then ask yourself, "How can I apply these thoughts, insights and /or ideas into my life and in my ministry? Include these insights into your journal

7. If you are in a small group, you may share your thoughts and insights using the "Invitation Method". Everyone is invited to share by name with the freedom to pass if they desire. If you are journaling alone, share your thoughts with a friend later.

8. Take time to contemplate on the Love of our Lord Jesus. Words are not necessary, just let God love you and speak to your heart in silence. (pause 10 minutes *).

9. Conclude with prayer. Thank God for the time with each other, thank God for the graces received, ask for help to appreciate diversity and to be a more inclusive person.

10. The goal of us gathering is to share, and become better instruments of unity and love in answer to the prayer of Jesus that we would all be one in the Lord

2.4 Prayer Old Covenant vs New Covenant Same God Same Faith

In the Bible, there is a clear distinction between the old covenant before the cross, and the new covenant after the cross. Under the old covenant, the children of Israel would only receive God's

blessings if they perfectly obeyed His commandments. The people attempted to be righteous through their works. By comparison, under the new covenant, we are blessed because we are in Christ Jesus." Righteousness is a gift we receive by faith in Him. The cross changed everything for us, including how we pray. Studying the Scriptures, we see that there is a difference between Old Testament prayer and New Testament prayer". (Creflo Dollar, Nov 2016)

The reason I included this information was one patient in the hospital confided in me that she had not read the old Testament for long time, because she was taught the old Testament was for Jewish people and not for Christians, so she neglected the Old Testament prayer, the psalms and the entire Bible passages. We have no idea how many of our brothers and sisters have been persuaded with erroneous opinions that our God never existed, we can only get the information through witnessing and evangelization by encountering one another, and how much the individual is willing to share with either a pastor, a minister, a Chaplain or other religious lay leaders.

In the Bible we were asked to pray without season. "Do not be anxious about anything, but in every situation do, with prayers and petitions, with thanksgiving, present your requests to God. ((NIV, Philippians. 4. 6-9.).

2.5 Prayer Square Small Group Gathering

Families that pray together stay together, and Jesus said, "Follow me, I will make you fishers of men. (NASB, Matthew. 4.19).

Table 1: PCM Prayer square small group gathering

Family Home: 2 names to lead prayer	Fellowship/Church: 10-12 members. Use the lectio divina model	Friends/School: Be descreet, witness during break
Park/Recreational time: Use discretion and play safe with fun.	Business: All work and no play makes Jack a dull boy. Loosen up and share Jesus with your group.	

Three Steps Process (see table 1)

The previous table depicts how the group gathering will open up the prayer square in a normal way with ease and peace.

1. Two names on each square
2. Select one person on each square to lead as spirit direct by pointing at someone to lead us into prayer
3. Do not forget to remind members, the date, time and confirm them coming.

2.6. Weekly Meeting Wednesday OR Friday toolbox

Table II: PCM Small group prayer and praise report 10-12 members

Date	Name	Prayer Request	Praise Report/ Update

Table III: PCM Small group roster and contact information

Name	Home Phone	Email

Table IV: PCM Small group calendar

(See table IV) below we use the calendar to track social events within the church, ministry projects, birthdays, wedding, etc. Our shared responsibilities and ownership ensures that responsibility for this group participation should not fall on one person alone. Facilitators will be rotated on weekly basis to ensure members' gifts of time and validation

Date	Lesson	Location/ Building	Faciliator	Snacks

Journals will be provided to record Bible passages, read with comments, reflection for individual members to carry to workshop and seminars at meeting each time.

2.7 How people pray during the Old Testament and in Jesus' Time

1. The men turned their faces away and went toward Sodom, but Abraham still stood before God. He asked God, will you destroy the righteous with the wicked? (NIV, Genesis 18. 22-23

a. Here, Abraham interceded for the people and pleaded with God to spare the city if a certain number of righteous people were found in it.

b. By comparison, when Jesus made intercession for us, He did not stop at just the apostles with Him that night. He asked God to spare everyone on earth, even if there were none righteous. (NIV, John. 17.1-5). We must pay close attention to verse2, in which Jesus said "For you granted Him authority over all people that

c. He might give eternal life to all those you have given Him" then in verse 20-25, He prayed for all believers. Only a loving, kind and peaceful God can do that.

d. Jesus became our settlement for sin. He made a perfect agreement between God and humanity and sealed it with His blood. If we can't talk to Jesus who else can we take our worries, anxieties and disappointment.

e. Some people still pray with a "before the cross" mindset, assuming this type of praying is still valid today. An example of this mindset is the belief that natural disasters are God's way of punishing people for their sins. Our Lord is not behind these, He is not behind these occurrences, because Jesus took care of sin for the entire world when He went on the cross.

f. When we make intercessory prayer, The Jabez prayer is an example of that simple and easy, straightforward, to the point, it was an Old Testament prayer but still effective today.   Here, we are reminding God of His saving grace and that if He did it for such and such, He can do it for us too. The intercessory prayer is a validation for God's Love and Grace in all of our lives, let's face it, He's the only one that can help, when everything fails. We rely on His providence and trust. The prayer of Jabez (NIV, 1 Chronicles. 4. 9-10.). "Oh, that you would bless me indeed, and enlarge my territory. That your hand would be with me, and that you would keep me from evil, that I may not cause pain". What a wonderful prayer it covers everything we need to say in any given prayers to the Lord with sincerity of heart.

2. Create in me a clean heart, O God, and renew a right spirit within me. Do not cast me away from your presence, and do not take your holy spirit from me (NIV, Psalm. 51.10, 11).

a. David was able to pray this, and we can because it is an Old Testament prayer. Faith of our father Holy Faith, their journey was a transitional to new testament. Jesus said before Moses. "I'm"

b. When we were born again, we became a new creation, and we were made perfectly clean. Our spirit became flawless then we were sealed with the Holy Spirit (NIV, Ephesians. 1.13).

c. God will never remove His Spirit from us. He has promised never to leave us (NIV, Hebrews. 13.:5,). Unless we told Him to take our name from book of life for disobeying Him, even that He will never leave us until we breathe our last breath, for initial judgement. Only Jesus can determine what punish to ascribe for work/deeds individual did while living, but He love so much.

A. New Testament prayer is powerful.

It is based on our identity in Christ (NIV, Matthew. 6.9-13).

9. "This, then, is how you should pray:

"'Our Father in heaven,

hallowed be your name,

10. your kingdom come,

your will be done,

on earth as it is in heaven.

11. Give us today our daily bread.

12. And forgive us our debts,
   as we also have forgiven our debtors.
13. And lead us not into temptation, [a]
   but deliver us from the evil one. [b]'

Footnotes:
a. Matthew 6:13
b. Matthew 6:13

B. Prayer Promises by God.

1. Our body is a temple of the Holy Spirit Who is inside us. We are not our own (NIV, 1 Corinthians. 6.19).

   a. We never have to worry whether our prayers will be hindered, because God is living inside us.

2. Jesus summoned His twelve disciples to Him and gave them power and authority over unclean spirits, to drive them out, and to cure diseases, weaknesses, and infirmities. He said to heal the sick, raise the dead, and drive out demons. Freely you have received, freely you give (NIV, Matthew. 10.1-8).

   a. Prayer is for building our relationship with God and communing with Him, but there is a difference between prayer and standing on our authority as Believers. We must not get the two confused.

   b. Sometimes we pray and talk to God about our problem when we should be using our power and authority to talk to the problem directly (NIV, Mark. 11.23).

3. I heard of your faith in Jesus, and I do not cease to give thanks for you, and pray that God may give you the spirit of wisdom and revelation in the knowledge of him (NIV, Ephesians. 1. 15-23).

   a. Here, Paul was praying that the Believers would receive revelation of what has already happened because of Christ, and how powerful He is in them. Likewise, we need to realize how powerful

God is in our lives.

b. Wisdom is knowing what to do when we do not know what to do. (NIV, Matthew 7.7). "Ask and it shall be given to you; seek and you shall find, knock and the door will be opened to you".

4. I exhort that prayers, intercessions, and thanksgiving be made for everyone, and for all who are in authority. This is good and acceptable in the sight of God, who wants everyone to be saved and come to the knowledge of the truth (ESV 1 Timothy 2.1-6).

a. Grace is the truth of which God wants us to have knowledge. Jesus brought grace and truth (ESV, John 1.17). When we come to know this truth, it will set us free (NIV, John 8.32-59).

5. The mystery the Scriptures refer to is that Christ is in us, and we are in Him. (NIV, Colossians. 4.1-6). (NIV, Colossians. 1. 26-27.) He now lived His life through us.

a. The mysteries are our redemption, holiness, perfection, and righteousness without our self-efforts. Once we receive a revelation of who we are in Christ, it is no longer a mystery.

6. Death and life are in the power of the tongue, and they that love it will eat of its fruits (ESV, Proverbs 18.21).

a. There is power in our prayers, and we must be careful how we pray. We can unleash this power for good or evil. Therefore, we must not complain or get negative when praying.

7. The joy of the Lord is your strength: (NASB, Nehemiah .8.10).

We must read this passage and understand where the Israelites are coming from. Their lives they found out was more than brick and mortar, it is not how successful you are that determine how relevant you are, you can be success yet insignificant in the society God Almighty place you, it is my pray for every human being walking this face of Earth to be relevant in their pursuit/endeavors.

The most important thing we have to worry about is our relationship to the Almighty Father who created us making us in His image and Likeness of God. The Israelites had just spent 70 years in Babylonian in captivity, yet their distress unspeakable, see (NASB, Nehemiah. 9.5-7).

By virtue of our inner connectedness our souls validate and become receptive to God's grace in us and then we capture the essence of Our Lord in our souls. "We are indeed born again". Prayer is the key to God's answering all our questions, whether in good times and in the worst of times.

Chapter 3:
King Solomon A King And A Prophet
(NASB, 1 King. 3. 5, 7-12). FULL-TEXT

3 Now Solomon loved the Lord, walking in the statutes of his father David, except he sacrificed and burned incense on the high places. 4 The king went to Gibeon to sacrifice there, for that was the great high place; Solomon offered a thousand burnt offerings on that altar. 5 In Gibeon the Lord appeared to Solomon in a dream at night; and God said, "Ask what you wish Me to give you."

Solomon's Prayer

6 Then Solomon said, "You have shown great lovingkindness to Your servant David my father, according as he walked before You in [b]truth and righteousness and uprightness of heart toward You; and You have [c]reserved for him this great lovingkindness, that You have given him a son to sit on his throne, as it is this day. 7 Now, O Lord my God, you have made Your servant king in place of my father David, yet I am but a little child; I do not know how to go out or come in. 8 Your servant is in the midst of Your people which You have chosen, a great people who are too many to be numbered or counted. 9 So give Your servant [d]an understanding heart to judge Your people to discern between good and evil. For who is able to judge this [e]great people of Yours?"

God's Answer

10 It was pleasing in the sight of the Lord that Solomon had asked this thing. 11 God said to him, "Because you have asked this thing and have not asked for yourself long life, nor have asked riches for yourself, nor have you asked for the life of your enemies, but have asked for yourself discernment to understand justice, 12 behold, and

I have done according to your words. Behold, I have given you a wise and discerning heart, so that there has been no one like you before you, nor shall one like you arise after you. 13 I have also given you what you have not asked, both riches and honor, so that there will not be any among the kings like you all your days. 14 If you walk in My ways, keeping My statutes and commandments, as your father David walked, then I will prolong your days."

15 Then Solomon awoke, and behold, it was a dream. And he came to Jerusalem and stood before the ark of the covenant of the Lord, and offered burnt offerings and made peace offerings, and made a feast for all his servants.

Solomon found favor with God, so can we. Look at this story and see which one mirror your own lives and run with it. We can be super rich and super talent, or simply in the middle. Our God uses us with what we got, we ought to stop and not blame ourselves and one another. Instead we say, Lord Look at me, take whatever you need today and bless me after you're done with me.

Footnotes:
a. 1 Kings 3:6
b. 1 Kings 3:6
c. 1 Kings 3:9
d. 1 Kings 3:10
e. 1 Kings 3:11
f. 1 Kings 3:12
g. 1 Kings 3:13

3.1 The Tower of Babel
(NASB, GENESIS. 11. 1-9 FULL-TEXT)

11 At one time all the people of the world spoke the same language and used the same words. 2 As the people migrated to the east, they

found a plain in the land of Babylonia and settled there.

3 They began saying to each other, "Let's make bricks and harden them with fire." (In this region bricks were used instead of stone, and tar was used for mortar.) 4 Then they said, "Come, let's build a great city for ourselves with a tower that reaches into the sky. This will make us famous and keep us from being scattered all over the world."

5 But the Lord came down to look at the city and the tower the people were building. 6 "Look!" he said. "The people are united, and they all speak the same language. After this, nothing they set out to do will be impossible for them! 7 Come, let's go down and confuse the people with different languages. Then they won't be able to understand each other."

8 In that way, the Lord scattered them all over the world, and they stopped building the city. 9 That is why the city was called Babel,] because that is where the Lord confused the people with different languages. In this way he scattered them all over the world.

3.2 The Discussion:

To fully appreciate this passage, the Israelites had just experienced the worst disaster known to man, flooding and they were just coming out of it, so there was re-building that must take place, they were bold, arrogant, v4 said what the people had in mind to isolate others and make the neighborhood Elitist" and they did not consult God with prayers, that they are ready to re-built.

They have forgotten their spiritual heritage. They built the tallest building with sound-proofed skyscrapers, they have indeed made it, they can do everything, they have just settled down in a comfort Zone of their own choosing, they kept God outside of their deliberation, but that day became the "Movement of the people" A déjà vu" all over again they no longer can speak just their language but the whole world. When God said yes nobody can say no, He did not want the Israelites to settle in mediocre. He wanted to expand their territories, and His divine plan was to make them Children of many nations as was His plan for Abraham, "Father of many nations"

Our God has to fulfil the promise made to Abraham, even though the children never thought about it.

Do you know the promise God made for your parents, and the good Lord will fulfil that promise one way or the other, how is your life journey going right now, has the Heavenly Father fulfil that promise for you yet, or are sins keeping them away to fulfillment, prayers are the answers for unfulfilled promises made, Ask God to give your dreams back to you. He will do it.

3.3 Ruth and Naomi (ESV, Ruth 1.1-23). FULL-TEXT.

1- In the days when the judges ruled there was a famine in the land, and a man of Bethlehem in Judah went to sojourn in the country of Moab, he and his wife and his two sons. 2 The name of the man was Elimelech and the name of his wife Naomi, and the names of his two sons were Mahlon and Chilion. They were Ephrathites from Bethlehem in Judah. They went into the country of Moab and remained there. 3 But Elimelech, the husband of Naomi, died, and she was left with her two sons. 4 These took Moabite wives; the name of the one was Orpah and the name of the other Ruth. They lived there about ten years, 5 and both Mahlon and Chilion died, so that the woman was left without her two sons and her husband.

Ruth's Loyalty to Naomi: What a Mighty God we serve
6 Then she arose with her daughters-in-law to return from the country of Moab, for she had heard in the fields of Moab that the Lord had visited his people and given them food. 7 So she set out

from the place where she was with her two daughters-in-law, and they went on the way to return to the land of Judah. 8 But Naomi said to her two daughters-in-law, "Go, and return each of you to her mother's house. May the Lord deal kindly with you, as you have dealt with the dead and with me. 9 The Lord grants that you may find rest, each of you in the house of her husband!" Then she kissed them, and they lifted up their voices and wept. 10 And they said to her, "No, we will return with you to your people." 11 But Naomi said, "Turn back, my daughters; why will you go with me? Have I yet sons in my womb that they may become your husbands? 12 Turn back, my daughters; go your way, for I am too old to have a husband. If I should say I have hope, even if I should have a husband this night and should bear sons, 13 would you therefore wait till they were grown? Would you therefore refrain from marrying? No, my daughters, for it is exceedingly bitter to me for your sake that the hand of the Lord has gone out against me." 14 Then they lifted up their voices and wept again. And Orpah kissed her mother-in-law, but Ruth clung to her.

15 And she said, "See, your sister-in-law has gone back to her people and to her gods; return after your sister-in-law." 16 But Ruth said, "Do not urge me to leave you or to return from following you. For where you go I will go and where you lodge I will lodge. Your people shall be my people and your God my God. 17 Where you die I will die, and there will I be buried. May the Lord do so to me and more also if anything but death part me from you." 18 And when Naomi saw that she was determined to go with her, she said no more.

3.4 Naomi and Ruth Return

19 So the two of them went on until they came to Bethlehem. And when they came to Bethlehem, the whole town was stirred because of them. And the women said, "Is this Naomi?" 20 She said to them,

"Do not call me Naomi; call me Mara, for the Almighty has dealt very bitterly with me. 21 I went away full, and the Lord has brought me back empty. Why call me Naomi, when the Lord has testified against me and the Almighty has brought calamity upon me?"

22 So Naomi returned, and Ruth the Moabite her daughter-in-law with her, who returned from the country of Moab. And they came to Bethlehem at the beginning of barley harvest.

Footnotes:
a. *Ruth 1:20 Naomi means pleasant*
b. *Ruth 1:20 Mara means bitter*

3.5 Ruth Meet Boaz (NIV, RUTH. 2.2-23).

A story of friendship, allegiance, compassion, love, commitment

1 Now Naomi had ta relative of her husband's, a worthy man of the clan of Elimelech, whose name was Boaz? 2 And Ruth the Moabite said to Naomi, "Let me go to thefield and vglean among the ears of grain after him in whose sight I shall find favor." Andshe said to her, "Go, my daughter." 3 So she set out and went and gleaned in the field afterthe reapers, and she happened to come to the part of the field belonging to Boaz, who wasof the clan of Elimelech. 4 And behold, Boaz came from Bethlehem. And he said to the reapers, "The LORD be with you!" And they answered, "The LORD bless you." 5 Then Boazsaid to his young man who was in charge of the reapers, "Whose young woman is this?"6 And the servant who was in charge of the reapers answered, "She is the young Moabitewoman, ywho came back with Naomi from the country of Moab. 7 She said, 'Please let meglean and gather among the sheaves after the reapers.' So she came, and she hascontinued from early morning until now, except for a short rest."1

8 Then Boaz said to Ruth, "Now, listen, my daughter, do not go to

glean in another fieldor leave this one, but keep close to my young women. 9 Let your eyes be on the field that they are reaping and go after them. Have I not charged the young men not to touch you? And when you are thirsty, go to the vessels and drink what the young men have drawn."10 Then zshe fell on her face, bowing to the ground, and said to him, "Why have I foundfavor in your eyes, that you should take notice of me, since I am a foreigner?" 11 But Boazanswered her"All that you have done for your mother-in-law since the death of yourhusband has been fully told to me, and how you left your father and mother and yournative land and came to a people that you did not know before. 12 cThe LORD repay you forwhat you have done, and a full reward be given you by the LORD, the God of Israel, underwhose wings you have come to take refuge!" 13 Then she said, "I have found favor in youreyes, my lord, for you have comforted me and spoken kindly to your servant, though I amnot one of your servants."

14 And at mealtime Boaz said to her, "Come here and eat some bread and dip yourmorsel in the wine." So she sat beside the reapers, and he passed to her roasted grain. Andshe ate until eshe was satisfied, and she had some left over. 15 When she rose to glean, Boaz instructed his young men, saying, "Let her glean even among the sheaves, and do notreproach her. 16 And also pull out some from the bundles for her and leave it for her toglean, and do not rebuke her."

17 So she gleaned in the field until evening. Then she beat out what she had gleaned, andit was about an ephah2 of barley. 18 And she took it up and went into the city. Her mother-in-law saw what she had gleaned. She also brought out and gave her what food she had leftover fafter being satisfied. 19 And her mother-in-law said to her, "Where did you gleantoday? And where have you worked? Blessed be the man gwho took notice of you." So shetold her mother-in-law with whom she had worked and said, "The man's name withwhom I worked today is Boaz." 20 And Naomi said to her daughter-in-law, h"May he beblessed by the LORD, whose kindness has not forsaken

ithe living or the dead!" Naomi alsosaid to her, "The man is a close relative of ours, one of jour redeemers." 21 And Ruth theMoabite said, "Besides, he said to me, 'You shall keep close by my young men until theyhave finished all my harvest.'" 22 And Naomi said to Ruth, her daughter-in-law, "It is good, my daughter, that you go out with his young women, lest in another field you beassaulted." 23 So she kept close to the young women of Boaz, gleaning until the end of thebarley and wheat harvests. And she lived with her mother-in-law.

3.6 Boaz Redeems Ruth

4 Now Boaz had gone up to xthe gate and sat down there. And behold, the redeemer, of whom Boaz had spoken, came by. So, Boaz said, "Turn aside, friend; sit downhere." And he turned aside and sat down. 2 And he took ten men zof the elders of the cityand said, "Sit down here." So they sat down. 3 Then he said to the redeemer, "Naomi, whohas come back from the country of Moab, is selling the parcel of land that belonged to ourrelative Elimelech. 4 So I thought I would tell you of it and say, a'Buy it in the presence ofthose sitting here and in the presence of the elders of my people.' If you will redeem it, redeem it. But if you1 will not, tell me, that I may know, for there is no one besides you toredeem it and I come after you." And he said, "I will redeem it." 5 Then Boaz said, "Theday you buy the field from the hand of Naomi, you also acquire Ruth2 the Moabite, thewidow of the dead, in order bto perpetuate the name of the dead in his inheritance."6 cThen the redeemer said, "I cannot redeem it for myself, lest I impair my owninheritance. Take my right of redemption yourself, for I cannot redeem it."

7 dNow this was the custom in former times in Israel concerning redeeming andexchanging: to confirm a transaction, the one drew off his sandal and gave it to the other, and this was the manner of

attesting in Israel. 8 So when the redeemer said to Boaz, "Buy it for yourself," he drew off his sandal. 9 Then Boaz said to the elders and all the people, "You are witnesses this day that I have bought from the hand of Naomi all that belonged to Elimelech and all that belonged to e Chilion and to Mahlon. 10 Also Ruth the Moabite, the widow of Mahlon, I have bought to be my wife, f to perpetuate the name of the dead in his inheritance, that the name of the dead may not be cut off from among his brothers and from the gate of his native place. You are witnesses this day." 11 Then all the people who were g at the gate and the elders said, "We are witnesses. May the LORD make the woman, who is coming into your house, like Rachel and Leah, h who together i built up the house of Israel? May you act worthily in j Ephrathah and k be renowned in Bethlehem, 12 and may your house be like the house of Perez, l whom Tamar bore to Judah, because m of the offspring that the LORD will give you by this young woman."

3.7 Ruth and Boaz Marry

13 So Boaz took Ruth, and she became his wife. And he went in to her, n and the LORD gave her conception and she bore a son. 14 o Then the women said to Naomi, "Blessed be the LORD, who has not left you this day without p a redeemer, and may his name q be renowned in Israel! 15 He shall be to you a restorer of life and a nourisher of your old age, for your daughter-in-law who loves you, r who is more to you than seven sons, has given birth to him." 16 Then Naomi took the child and laid him on her lap and became his nurse. 17 s And the women of the neighborhood gave him a name, saying, "A son has been born to Naomi." They named him Obed. He was the father of Jesse, the father of David.

b. The Genealogy of David

18 Now these are the generations of Perez: t Perez fathered Hezron,

19 Hezron fathered Ram, Ram fathered Amminadab, 20 uAmminadab fathered Nahshon, Nahshon fatheredSalmon, 21 Salmon fathered Boaz, Boaz fathered Obed, 22 Obed fathered Jesse, and Jesse fathered David.

3.8 The Discussion:

We have to review the story of Ruth and Naomi to get the historical answer given by Peter to Jesus when the apostles assembled with Jesus before sending them out in pair, our Lord asked the apostles "Who thou sayeth Iam? Peter replied, "You are the Messiah, son of the Living God" (NIV, Matthew. 16.16).

Jesus recognized that the Father was at work in Simon, and He gave Him a new name "Peter" meaning Rock. Jesus declared that day "upon this rock I will build my church. I will give you the key to the "Kingdom of Heaven" (Matthew 16:18-19 NIV) by that pronunciation that day Peter became the head of the apostles. Again we remembered from our Bible recalled that Jacob too named was changed when He wrestled with an Angel, saying I will never let you go until you blessed me, that day too Jacob name was change to Israel-"Father of Many nations" Our Lord has been a persistent God, Never Ever changing God, who always give out your rewards when we earned them, just like this ultimate journey to Heaven, there are rewards to give out during judgement day, we must inform others about His Mercy and goodness of our Lord.

Peter was not the brightest or the strongest of the Apostles, he too was the weakest link, but Almighty Father sees our heart and He judges according to our worth. In His eyes we are equal; He has no respect for nobody. Apostles Paul reminded us too that he was not the brightest among the people and he prosecuted Christians before his conversion, so our Lord can take a hopeless situation and turn it into first class end-product.

The point I'm trying to make with story of Naomi and the question Jesus asked the apostles about His Sovereignty Naomi lost everything; Ruth has nowhere to go, married outside her tribe, broke and penniless. if she stayed with Naomi she will be safe, and the fact that she loved her mother-in-law so much as a human being, and while her husband Naomi son was alive they treated her very well, so this passage to me is about Love, friendship, loyalty and compassion.

And God's grace and Holy Spirit which always come to the children of God in the fruits of Holy Spirit in Joy, peace, kindness, forbearance, Love, gentleness, goodness, faithfulness and self-control emerged and was impacted to Ruth the moment she believed and followed Naomi with utterance "Your God is my God too". What a hope sealer-our Lord is, always and ever shall be for those who put their trust in Him.

CHAPTER 4:
God is Working for Us. Are You Working for God?

The moment we allow our enemies to dictate what we can eat, where to assemble or simply to take over our estate in life, we might as well tell God we have no fighting chance, pack up the ideas we have and abandon our projects, those beautiful projects He want us to explore. We as people, we challenge one another, but failed to challenge God, is okay to ask Him, Father God how will you do this? you think if I do it this way, there is a way in there? We have to honor God with the "Gift of Self and Time" meaning asking God to shed light into our daily activities, let our light shine so that we can be a blessing to others. Let's face it, our time here on Earth is short, and none of us is granted any day, we must do everything within our power to be kind and adopt a friendly union with God and each other. We must have an attitude of commitment, loyalty, passion, love and believe that God will make everything better for the good of His people. God always use one person at a time to benefit masses, which is why I have chosen these two passages to illustrate my point.

4.1 The Samaritan Woman
(NIV, JOHN. 4.1-42). FULL TEXT

1 Now Jesus learned that the Pharisees had heard that he was gaining and baptizing more disciples than John— 2 although in fact it was not Jesus who baptized, but his disciples. 3 So he left Judea and went back once more to Galilee.

4 Now he had to go through Samaria. 5 So he came to a town in Samaria called Sychar, near the plot of ground Jacob had given to his son Joseph. 6 Jacob's well was there, and Jesus, tired as he was from

the journey, sat down by the well. It was about noon.

7 When a Samaritan woman came to draw water, Jesus said to her, "Will you give me a drink?"8 (His disciples had gone into the town to buy food.)

9 The Samaritan woman said to him, "You are a Jew and I am a Samaritan woman. How can you ask me for a drink?" (For Jews do not associate with Samaritans.

10 Jesus answered her, "If you knew the gift of God and who it is that asks you for a drink, you would have asked him, and he would have given you living water."

11 "Sir," the woman said, "you have nothing to draw with and the well is deep. Where can you get this living water? 12 Are you greater than our father Jacob, who gave us the well and drank from it himself, as did also his sons and his livestock?"

13 Jesus answered, "Everyone who drinks this water will be thirsty again, 14 but whoever drinks the water I give them will never thirst. Indeed, the water I give them will become in them a spring of water welling up to eternal life."

15 The woman said to him, "Sir, give me this water so that I won't get thirsty and have to keep coming here to draw water."

16 He told her, "Go, call your husband and come back."

17 "I have no husband," she replied.

Jesus said to her, "You are right when you say you have no husband. 18 The fact is, you have had five husbands, and the man you now have is not your husband. What you have just said is quite true."

19 "Sir," the woman said, "I can see that you are a prophet. 20 Our ancestors worshiped on this mountain, but you Jews claim that the place where we must worship is in Jerusalem."

21 "Woman," Jesus replied, "believe me, a time is coming when you will worship the Father neither on this mountain nor in Jerusalem. 22 You Samaritans worship what you do not know; we worship what we do know, for salvation is from the Jews. 23 Yet a time is coming and

has now come when the true worshipers will worship the Father in the Spirit and in truth, for they are the kind of worshipers the Father seeks. 24 God is spirit, and his worshipers must worship in the Spirit and in truth."

25 The woman said, "I know that Messiah" (called Christ) "is coming. When he comes, he will explain everything to us."

26 Then Jesus declared, "I, the one speaking to you—I am he."

27 Just then his disciples returned and were surprised to find him talking with a woman. But no one asked, "What do you want?" or "Why are you talking with her?"

28 Then, leaving her water jar, the woman went back to the town and said to the people, 29 "Come, see a man who told me everything I ever did. Could this be the Messiah?" 30 They came out of the town and made their way toward him.

31 Meanwhile his disciples urged him, "Rabbi, eat something."

32 But he said to them, "I have food to eat that you know nothing about."

33 Then his disciples said to each other, "Could someone have brought him food?"

34 "My food," said Jesus "is to do the will of him who sent me and to finish his work. 35 Don't you have a saying, 'It's still four months until harvest'? I tell you, open your eyes and look at the fields! They are ripe for harvest. 36 Even now the one who reaps draws a wage and harvests a crop for eternal life, so that the sower and the reaper may be glad together. 37 Thus the saying 'One sows and another reaps' is true. 38 I sent you to reap what you have not worked for. Others have done the hard work, and you have reaped the benefits of their labor."

39 Many of the Samaritans from that town believed in him because of the woman's testimony, "He told me everything I ever did." 40 So when the Samaritans came to him, they urged him to stay with them, and he stayed two days. 41 And because of his words many more became believers.

42 They said to the woman, "We no longer believe just because of what you said; now we have heard for ourselves, and we know that this man really is the Savior of the world."

4.2 The Discussion

What a mighty God we serve the service of ONE for many. What a spiritual Awakening for the town people. The people of Samaritan that day have no clue, Jesus was coming to their town for faith formation, the first of its kind. A revival and A retreat with the Apostles. Jesus did not need an invitation to visit you and I. He's the King of Kings, Lord of Lords, our Savior, and our Redeemer.

Jesus our Divine Listener who allows men and women to be awakened with time, and stay there till end of-time to answer questions, and continues to provides inspirations and guidance for those who called upon Him.

His journey continues with each and every one of us. "Salvation is a gift God gives to those who believe. We cannot earn it, we are imperfect, and we cannot make ourselves perfect. Yet God demands perfection, therefore, all we can do is cast ourselves on God's Mercy. In His Mercy God offers to forgive our sins and give us a new nature of Holiness, so that we can be in perfect relationship with Him" (Ander 235).

God uses the weakest link in a group to make a statement which will benefit our souls. His ultimate goal for us His children is to have light at the end of the tunnel, our ultimate goal is to end up in God's Kingdom, and He told us to be vigilant and work smart,

He told us to check His public teachings, parables, healing gatherings and words of encouragements in His sacred text, and He wanted none of us should be deprived of His Grace or have any excuse not to read His Holy Bible which contains a lot of information for our lives journey, we have to come under His grace to activate that "Living Water" or "Well" in each and every one of us, His Divine nature compel us to do so

The passage each time I read it I Asked myself, what is our Lord trying to do, and each time I posed the question new message comes up, this meant the Word of our Lord is everlasting, each person can analysis it over and over with different angle and yet arrive to the same conclusion of His saving grace.

Here in this passage the word Love, compassion, hope, loyalty and freedom all wrapped up as one. The passage is divided into multiples part, we have Jesus, the woman, the disciples, the townspeople, God the Father,

The well owned by Jacob, the father of Israelites and the scene, if we picture the weather that day it would have been very hot, so the stage was set in its natural form, just like our God was on Stage during the creation of the universe.

Here now, a small town. Jesus picked this town for His first retreat. The woman quickly figured Jesus out that He must be a prophet because everything that ever happened to her, Jesus knew about them, how many of us pretend our Lord never knows nothing about us, it is high time we stop that notion, He created us, breathe His breath unto us for life. Jesus came to save us from our sins and spiritual dryness, just like them.

The woman asked Jesus how can you ask me for a drink and Jesus replied "If only you recognized God's gift, and who it is that is asking you for a drink, you would have asked him instead, and He would have given you a "Living Water" and during the conversation again, Jesus said "Everyone who drinks this water –meaning the well will be thirsty again, "But whoever drinks the water I give him, will never be thirsty."

Verse 21-23 hit the home run for me, "yet an hour is coming and is already here, when worshipers will worship the Father in Spirit and truth. Jesus just told the woman His future plan for us.He told her true believers will never has to come to this mountain again and worship, whosoever believes, Jesus Spirit will continue to dwell in their hearts forever, Jesus revealed himself to this woman that day, and the real counselor, our advocate, Holy Spirit, the completion of Triune God right there. We also remembered that during the "Tower of Babel" language had changed to many languages of the world, there were movement of people from regions to regions, so the good Lord already initiated the process, Jesus again came to that township for them to start moving as well, most of them were still stocked in the old way of doing business which can impede growth and stability. The people of Samaritan rediscovered themselves and started living in the present not in the past. They accepted Jesus Christ as their Lord and Savior.

Serious evangelization took place by Jesus and the Apostle for two days they stayed, ate with them, toured the town, fellowship with them, one thing that I got from reading this passage was Our Lord validated the original owner of the well- "Jacob." Jesus told Peter someone in the past had planted the seeds, now the apostles came to reap what had been sowed. Blessings through the faith of one person. We got the inferment through the dialogue with the Samaritan woman and Jesus.

Our Lord visited that town that day was not an accident, He was making round to touch His base, knowing He will never pass through Samaritan township again. We will have to trust Him enough to place our lives in His Keep, after all when our souls lives our bodies, we have no control either for this present time or the next life, but we pray that Jesus hands will be all over us, to take our souls to His Kingdom and not the enemy. Amen

4.3 The Transfiguration (NIV, Luke. 9. 29-36).

29 As he was praying, the appearance of his face changed, and his clothes became as bright as a flash of lightning. 30 Two men, Moses and Elijah, appeared in glorious splendor, talking with Jesus. 31 They spoke about his departure,[a] which he was about to bring to fulfillment at Jerusalem. 32 Peter and his companions were very sleepy, but when they became fully awake, they saw his glory and the two men standing with him. 33 As the men were leaving Jesus, Peter said to him, "Master, it is good for us to be here. Let us put up three shelters—one for you, one for Moses and one for Elijah." (He did not know what he was saying.)

34 While he was speaking, a cloud appeared and covered them, and they were afraid as they entered the cloud. 35 A voice came from the cloud, saying, "This is my Son, whom I have chosen; listen to him." 36 When the voice had spoken, they found that Jesus was alone. The disciples kept this to themselves and did not tell anyone at that time what they had seen.

Footnotes:
a. Luke 9:31 Greek exodos

4.4 Unity in the Body of Christ (ESV, Ephesians. 4.1-32).

4 I therefore, a prisoner for the Lord, urge you to walk in a manner worthy of the calling to which you have been called, 2 with all humility and gentleness, with patience, bearing with one another in love, 3 eager to maintain the unity of the Spirit in the bond of peace. 4 There is one body and one Spirit—just as you were called to the one hope that belongs to your call— 5 one Lord, one faith, one baptism, 6 one God and Father of all, who is over all and through all and in all.

7 But grace was given to each one of us according to the measure of Christ's gift.8 Therefore it says,

"When he ascended on high he led a host of captives, and he gave gifts to men."[a]

9 (In saying, "He ascended," what does it mean but that he had also descended into the lower regions, the earth?[b] 10 He who descended is the one who also ascended far above all the heavens, that he might fill all things.) 11 And he gave the apostles, the prophets, the evangelists, the shepherds[c] and teachers,[d] 12 to equip the saints for the work of ministry, for building up the body of Christ, 13 until we all attain to the unity of the faith and of the knowledge of the Son of God, to mature manhood,[e] to the measure of the stature of the fullness of Christ, 14 so that we may no longer be children, tossed to and fro by the waves and carried about by every wind of doctrine, by human cunning, by craftiness in deceitful schemes. 15 Rather, speaking the truth in love, we are to grow up in every way into him who is the head, into Christ,16 from whom the whole body, joined and held together by every joint with which it is equipped, when each part is working properly, makes the body grow so that it builds itself up in love.

17 Now this I say and testify in the Lord, that you must no longer walk as the Gentiles do, in the futility of their minds. 18 They are darkened in their understanding, alienated from the life of God because of the ignorance that is in them, due to their hardness of heart. 19 They have become callous and have given themselves up to sensuality, greedy to practice every kind of impurity. 20 But that is not the way you learned Christ!— 21 assuming that you have heard about him and were taught in him, as the truth is in Jesus, 22 to put off your old self,[f] which belongs to your former manner of life and is corrupt through deceitful desires,23 and to be renewed in the spirit of your minds, 24 and to put on the new self, created after the likeness of God in true righteousness and holiness.

25 Therefore, having put away falsehood, let each one of you speak

the truth with his neighbor, for we are members one of another. 26 Be angry and do not sin; do not let the sun go down on your anger, 27 and give no opportunity to the devil. 28 Let the thief no longer steal, but rather let him labor, doing honest work with his own hands, so that he may have something to share with anyone in need. 29 Let no corrupting talk come out of your mouths, but only such as is good for building up, as fits the occasion, that it may give grace to those who hear. 30 And do not grieve the Holy Spirit of God, by whom you were sealed for the day of redemption. 31 Let all bitterness and wrath and anger and clamor and slander be put away from you, along with all malice. 32 Be kind to one another, tenderhearted, forgiving one another, as God in Christ forgave you.

Footnotes:
a. Ephesians 4: 8
b. Ephesians 4: 9
c. Ephesians 4: 11
d. Ephesians 4 :11
e. Ephesians 4: 13
f. Ephesians 4: 22

4.5 The Discussion and importance of the two Bible passages Jesus Identity (NASB,Luke. 9. 28-36.) (ESV, Ephesians. 4.1-32).

The Lord was exactly doing what He promised us in (NASB, Ezekiel. 34. 11-16.).

Moses was a great person, a prophet whom God Almighty used for salvation of the Israelites and the gentiles, he worked for God and took his vocation very serious, through Moses God gave us the ten commandments, since then no prophet has risen in Israel or any other nations that could see God face –to-face and lived to talk about it.

In (ESV, Exodus. 24. 3-8). We read how Moses performed all rituals and ordinances of our God with humility and care, and the people of Israelites took Moses seriously and responded well with the words of God.

Christ interacted on daily basis with the Apostles , and one day He asked this question, "Who do people say that the son of man is,? v14 said" Some say John the Baptist; and others Elijah; but still others, Jeremiah, or one of the prophets."v15He said to them , "But who do you say that Iam?"v16 Simon Peter answered, "You are the Christ, the son of the Living God." Our Lord has to do something quick for His Apostles to get it that He was not Just one of them, but He had to convinced them that He was more than that and to help Peter with that proclamation, that indeed God Almighty was in their midst.

I will go further and use a marketing strategy for clarity sake under product identification. Jesus is the product, not to domesticate Our Lord but to make this point clear. One of the biggest arsenal the marketers used is product labeling which include, brand product, protection under constant threats from theft and counterfeit products.

Our Lord was, is and yet to come a" big item", if not protected could fall into wrong hand, some Apostle thought He was just a Rabbi, Elijah, in other to stop the confusion. He took James, John and Peter to mount of Transfiguration for them to see for themselves that He was not making Himself up or playing them for a fool, He wanted them to know that indeed He is our Lord and our savior. Same thing the Samaritan woman did not know who Jesus was, but heard from elders and the story of God passed down from generation unto generation that God is omnipotent and omnipresence, she believed, and Jesus did not want to exclude them (Township) from His grace, our Lord is God of inclusion, whether you're born slaves, Jews or Gentiles you're included., Jesus hand picked three disciples to see the old Jerusalem and the new Jerusalem, meaning the transition of power to relieve Moses and Elijah their duties and welcoming the new Apostles who will from now on carry the touch. Apostle Paul joined them later, Our God never make mistakes, our future he's already there before us-Amen, Amen. All Christians the moment we pick up our crosses to follow Him, we are representing Jesus, if the Apostles got it, we too will get. The mount of Transfiguration was very important to Christians. He gave the Law to Moses on Mount Sanai and before Jesus could modified the new commandments into two workable components in the new testament, the carrier and the champion of the original ten commandments who presented the Israelites our God's ways of life, the real law man must be present and the Prophet who pray always that we keep the law must also be present. In (NASB, Matthew. 22. 6-40 NASB). Jesus responded to the question posted at him by his Disciples.

36 "Teacher, which is the great commandment in the Law?" 37 And He said to him, "'You shall love the Lord your God with all your heart, and with all your soul, and with all your mind.' 38 This is the great and [a]foremost commandment. 39 The second is like it, 'You shall love your neighbor as yourself.' 40 On these two commandments depend the whole Law and the Prophets."

On the mount of Transfiguration, Moses and Elijah appeared, Moses representing Law, and Elijah His prophet. Elijah always intervened whenever God's people are threatened. Elijah helped the Israelites that Yahweh guided the fortunes of the nations, and that other gods were under the control of Almighty God. Yahweh not Baal had the power of life and death, Elijah taught the Israelites that it was not in bad times that God responded but during good times also. And who can forget the Voice to the three Apostles who went with our Lord. "v35 This is my son, my chosen one, listen to Him".   Then Apostles Paul confronted the people of Ephesus to take their vocations serious and not take it for granted and watch out for worldly things, he told them to be careful and watch out for lots of chiefs no Indians that they should work in unity for common purpose, in other word take care of the gifts God gave them.

4.6 The Five Selected Parables of Jesus with Connection to Heaven.

1. The Parable of the Weeds (ESV, Matthew. 13.24-30).

24 He put another parable before them, saying, "The kingdom of heaven may be compared to a man who sowed good seed in his field, 25 but while his men were sleeping, his enemy came and sowed weeds[a] among the wheat and went away. 26 So when the plants came up and bore grain, then the weeds appeared also. 27 And the servants[b] of the master of the house came and said to him, 'Master, did you not sow good seed in your field? How then does it have weeds?' 28 He said to them, 'An enemy has done this.' So, the servants said to him, 'Then do you want us to go and gather them?' 29 But he said, 'No, lest in gathering the weeds you root up the wheat along with them. 30 Let both grow together until the harvest, and at harvest time I will tell the reapers, "Gather the weeds first and bind them in bundles to be burned but gather the wheat into my barn."'"

b. The Tares Explained

36 Then He left the crowds and went into the house. And His disciples came to Him and said, "Explain to us the parable of the [b] tares of the field." 37 And He said, "The one who sows the good seed is the Son of Man, 38 and the field is the world; and as for the good seed, these are the sons of the kingdom; and the tares are the sons of the evil one;39 and the enemy who sowed them is the devil, and the harvest is the [c]end of the age; and the reapers are angels. 40 So just as the tares are gathered up and burned with fire, so shall it be at the [d] end of the age.41 The Son of Man will send forth His angels, and they will gather out of His kingdom [e]all stumbling blocks, and those who

commit lawlessness,42 and will throw them into the furnace of fire; in that place there will be weeping and gnashing of teeth. 43 Then the righteous will shine forth as the son in the kingdom of their Father. He who has ears, [f]let him hear.

Footnotes:
a. *Matthew 13:25*
b. *Matthew 13:27*

2. A Dragnet (NASB, Matthew. 13. 47-50).

47 "Again, the kingdom of heaven is like a dragnet cast into the sea and gathering fish of every kind; 48 and when it was filled, they drew it up on the beach; and they sat down and gathered the good fish into containers, but the bad they threw away. 49 So it will be at the [a]end of the age; the angels will come forth and [b]take out the wicked from among the righteous, 50 and will throw them into the furnace of fire; in that day there will be weeping and gnashing of teeth.

3. Parable of the Guests (NASB, Luke. 7.7-15).

7 And He began speaking a parable to the invited guests when He noticed how they had been picking out the places of honor at the table, saying to them, 8 "When you are invited by someone to a wedding feast, do not [e]take the place of honor, for someone more distinguished than you may have been invited by him, 9 and he who invited you both will come and say to you, 'Give your place to this man,' and then in disgrace you [f]proceed to occupy the last place. 10 But when you are invited, go and recline at the last place, so that when the one who has invited you comes, he may say to you, 'Friend, move up higher'; then you will have honor in the sight of all who [g] are at the table with you. 11 For everyone who exalts himself will be

humbled, and he who humbles himself will be exalted."

12 And He also went on to say to the one who had invited Him, "When you give a luncheon or a dinner, do not invite your friends or your brothers or your relatives or rich neighbors, otherwise they may also invite you in return and that will be your repayment. 13 But when you give a [h]reception, invite the poor, the crippled, the lame, the blind, 14 and you will be blessed, since they [i]do not have the means to repay you; for you will be repaid at the resurrection of the righteous."

15 When one of those who were reclining at the table with Him heard this, he said to Him, "Blessed is everyone who will eat bread in the kingdom of God!"

4. Parable of the Diner (NASB, Luke. 7.16-24).

16 But He said to him, "A man was giving a big dinner, and he invited many; 17 and at the dinner hour he sent his slave to say to those who had been invited, 'Come; for everything is ready now.' 18 But they all alike began to make excuses. The first one said to him, 'I have bought a [j]piece of land and I need to go out and look at it; [k] please consider me excused.' 19 Another one said, 'I have bought five yoke of oxen, and I am going to try them out; [l]please consider me excused.' 20 Another one said, 'I have married a wife, and for that reason I cannot come.' 21 And the slave came back and reported this to his master. Then the head of the household became angry and said to his slave, 'Go out at once into the streets and lanes of the city and bring in here the poor and crippled and blind and lame.' 22 And the slave said, 'Master, what you commanded has been done, and still there is room.' 23 And the master said to the slave, 'Go out into the highways and along the hedges, and compel them to come in, so that my house may be filled. 24 For I tell you, none of those men who were invited shall taste of my dinner.'"

5. Laborers in the Vineyard (ESV, Matthew. 20:1-16).

20 "For the kingdom of heaven is like a master of a house who went out early in the morning to hire laborers for his vineyard. 2 After agreeing with the laborers for a denarius[a] a day, he sent them into his vineyard. 3 And going out about the third hour he saw others standing idle in the marketplace, 4 and to them he said, 'You go into the vineyard too, and whatever is right I will give you.' 5 So they went. Going out again about the sixth hour and the ninth hour, he did the same. 6 And about the eleventh hour he went out and found others standing. And he said to them, 'Why do you stand here idle all day?' 7 They said to him, 'Because no one has hired us.' He said to them, 'You go into the vineyard too.' 8 And when evening came, the owner of the vineyard said to his foreman, 'Call the laborers and pay them their wages, beginning with the last, up to the first.' 9 And when those hired about the eleventh hour came, each of them received a denarius. 10 Now when those hired first came, they thought they would receive more, but each of them also received a denarius. 11 And on receiving it they grumbled at the master of the house, 12 saying, 'These last worked only one hour, and you have made them equal to us who have borne the burden of the day and the scorching heat.' 13 But he replied to one of them, 'Friend, I am doing you no wrong. Did you not agree with me for a denarius? 14 Take what belongs to you and go. I choose to give to this last worker as I give to you. 15 Am I not allowed to do what I choose with what belongs to me? Or do you begrudge my generosity?'[b] 16 So the last will be first, and the first last."

Footnotes:
a. *Matthew 20:2 A denarius was a day's wage for a laborer*
b. *Matthew 20:15 is your eye bad because I am good?*

4.7 Why Did Jesus Speak in Parables?

One of the methods Jesus employed in communicating His message was through parables. A parable is basically an earthly story with a heavenly meaning. When Jesus started telling parables to the people, His disciples asked the obvious question, "Why do You speak to them in parables?" (NASB, Matthew. 10. 13).

Because it has been given to you to know the mysteries of the kingdom of heaven, but to them it has not been given. And in them the prophecy of Isaiah is fulfilled, which says: 'Hearing you will hear and shall not understand, and seeing you will see and not perceive, for the heart of this people has grown dull. Their ears are hard of hearing, and their eyes they have closed, lest they should see with their eyes and hear with their ears, lest they should understand with their heart and turn, so that I should heal them' (NASB, Matthew.13.11,14,15).

Unwillingness on the part of the people to receive Jesus' message of the kingdom was the reason that He taught in parables. The truths of the kingdom of God were heard by them but not understood. It was not because God was hiding the truth from them-it was because they did not want to hear. We read in the parable of the Laborers how our Lord generosity extended to even the late comers to His vineyards. The owner we were told paid the same amount of wages from start of the dawn to the newcomers, they disputed but Jesus has the last word by saying to them, we are all equal in His sight. His generosity and Mercy to us all by inviting us to sit at the table with Him.

God has given the people every chance to accept the message of Jesus. His ministry was attested by miracles. He offered the proper credentials as the Messiah, yet they did not believe Him. The realities of the kingdom, therefore, were not theirs to know. "The people who believed in Jesus as the Messiah would understand the parables. They would comprehend the great truths of the kingdom of God. The scripture must be spiritually look at and believe". (Don Stewart).

Apostle Paul said, "But we speak the wisdom of God in a mystery, the hidden wisdom which God ordained before the ages for our glory, which none of the rulers of this age knew; for had they known they would not have crucified the Lord of glory... For what man knows the things of man except the spirit of the man which is in him? Even so no one knows the things of God except the Spirit of God... But the natural man does not receive the things of the Spirit of God, for they are foolishness to him; nor can he know them, because they are spiritually discerned (NASB, 1 Corinthians. 2.7, 8, 11, 14).). Therefore, most people were not interested in the truth during Jesus time. But now, each and every one of us must try to lead the way to the cross.

Therefore, I speak to them in parables, because seeing they do not see, and hearing they do not hear, nor do they understand (NASB, Matthew. 13.13). Jesus spoke in parables earthly stories with heavenly meaning. He did so that His disciples would comprehend His teachings and that unbelievers would be without comprehension. Those interested in understanding the truth of His message would understand and seek for them to understand the meaning of His coming to Earth, while those not interested would remain without understanding and not seek to educate themselves before the owner of the Vineyard comes back.

4.8 Faith of our Mothers Holy Faith Project Picked Five Women from the Bible

1. Miriam (NASB, Exodus. 15.19-21). We praise your name Miriam who sang triumphantly while Pharaoh's vaunted army laid drowned beneath the Red Sea, As Israelites marched to freedom. Their chains of bondage gone, so may we reach the Kingdom your mighty arm won for us God and our Savior.

2. Hannah (NASB, 1 Samuel. 1.1-2.10). We sang to Hannah, who

prayed without child before your throne of grace, but rewarded her with Samuel to serve before your face. Lord Jesus grant each and every one of us her perseverance how to pray and trust in your deliverance when we are in doubt, hopeless, helpless and in fear.

3. Martha and Mary (NIV, Luke. 10.38-42). We read about Martha in the Bible who toiled with pot and pan, while her little sister Mary sat in silence to hear what our Lord got to say over and over, and Jesus told Martha, nobody will deprived Mary of the grace of our Lord, because she chose well. Lord keep our hearts attentive to your truth and strengthen us for service when work becomes our prayer.

4. Mary, Mother of our Lord (NIV, Luke. 1. 26-38). All Christians honor faithful Mary the first Apostle, Fair maiden, full of grace. She bore Christ, our Savior who saved us from jaw of death. May each and every one of us surrender ourselves to His commands and lay upon the altar our gifts of hearts and hands to serve Jesus, and each other's, and gain our seats for well earn sacrifice here on Earth in His Kingdom.

5. Mary Magdalene (New King James Version, John. 20 .1-18). We praise Mary one of the females in our Lord ministry who believed every teaching, parables, doctrines and went with the twelves to all rallies, retreats and revivals, she was also there at the foot of the cross with His Mother, and on the Easter morning went with other females in our Lord's ministry according to Jewish customs to apply burial balm/oils to Jesus' body but found the stone had been rolled, but very nearby saw Him our Lord in His resurrected light. May we by faith behold our Lord's when our own light ends to follow Him to Paradise, just like He promised the thief who was with Him on the cross that faithful day. "Today you will be with me in paradise".

CHAPTER 5:
The Birth of Jesus Christ Foretold:
(NIV, LUKE. 1. 26-33).

26 In the sixth month of Elizabeth's pregnancy, God sent the angel Gabriel to Nazareth, a town in Galilee,

27 to a virgin pledged to be married to a man named Joseph, a descendant of David. The virgin's name was Mary.

28 The angel went to her and said, "Greetings, you who are highly favored! The Lord is with you."

29 Mary was greatly troubled at his words and wondered what kind of greeting this might be.

30 But the angel said to her, "Do not be afraid, Mary; you have found favor with God.

31 You will conceive and give birth to a son, and you are to call him Jesus.

32 He will be great and will be called the Son of the Most High. The Lord God will give him the throne of his father David,

33 and he will reign over Jacob's descendants forever; his kingdom will never end."

5.1 Mary's Song (NASB, Luke. 1.46-56)

The Magnificat: Mary song

46 And Mary said:

"My soul]exalts the Lord,

47 And my spirit has rejoiced in God my Savior.

48 "For He has had regard for the humble state of His [b]bond slave;

For behold, from this time on all generations will count me blessed.

49 "For the Mighty One has done great things for me;

And holy is His name.

50 "And His mercy is]upon generation after generation

Toward those who fear Him.

51 "He has done]mighty deeds with His arm;

He has scattered those who were proud in the]thoughts of their heart.

52 "He has brought down rulers from their thrones,

And has exalted those who were humble.

53 "He has filled the hungry with good things;

And sent away the rich empty-handed.

54 "He has given help to Israel His servant,

[f]In remembrance of His mercy,

55 As He spoke to our fathers,

To Abraham and his descendants forever."

56 And Mary stayed with her about three months, and then returned to her home.

5.2 The Word Became Flesh Our Messiah on Stage (NIV, John. 1.1-18)

1 In the beginning was the Word, and the Word was with God, and the Word was God. 2 He was in the beginning with God. 3 All things were made through him, and without him was not anything made that was made. 4 In him was life,[a] and the life was the light of men. 5 The light shines in the darkness, and the darkness has not overcome it.

6 There was a man sent from God, whose name was John. 7 He came as a witness, to bear witness about the light, that all might believe through him. 8 He was not the light, but came to bear witness about the light.

9 The true light, which gives light to everyone, was coming into

the world. 10 He was in the world, and the world was made through him, yet the world did not know him. 11 He came to his own,[b] and his own people[c] did not receive him. 12 But to all who did receive him, who believed in his name, he gave the right to become children of God,13 who were born, not of blood nor of the will of the flesh nor of the will of man, but of God.

14 And the Word became flesh and dwelt among us, and we have seen his glory, glory as of the only Son[d] from the Father, full of grace and truth. 15 (John bore witness about him, and cried out, "This was he of whom I said, 'He who comes after me ranks before me, because he was before me.'") 16 For from his fullness we have all received, grace upon grace.[e] 17 For the law was given through Moses; grace and truth came through Jesus Christ. 18 No one has ever seen God; the only God,[f] who is at the Father's side,[g] he has made him known.

5.3 The Lamb of God
(NIV, JOHN. 1. 29-34)

29 The next day John saw Jesus coming toward him and said, "Look, the Lamb of God, who takes away the sin of the world! 30 This is the one I meant when I said, 'A man who comes after me has surpassed me because he was before me.' 31 I myself did not know him, but the reason I came baptizing with water was that he might be revealed to Israel."

32 Then John gave this testimony: "I saw the Spirit come down from heaven as a dove and remain on him. 33 And I myself did not know him, but the one who sent me to baptize with water told me, 'The man on whom you see the Spirit come down and remain is the one who will baptize with the Holy Spirit.' 34 I have seen, and I testify that this is God's Chosen One.

5.4 Jesus First Miracle with Mary's Help
(NIV, JOHN. 2.1-8)

The Wedding at Cana

2 On the third day there was a wedding at Cana in Galilee, and the mother of Jesus was there. 2 Jesus also was invited to the wedding with his disciples. 3 When the wine ran out, the mother of Jesus said to him, "They have no wine." 4 And Jesus said to her, "Woman, what does this have to do with me? My hour has not yet come." 5 His mother said to the servants, "Do whatever he tells you."

6 Now there were six stone water jars there for the Jewish rites of purification, each holding twenty or thirty gallons.[a] 7 Jesus said to the servants, "Fill the jars with water." And they filled them up to the brim.8 And he said to them, "Now draw some out and take it to the master of the feast." So, they took it.

5.5 Jesus Arrested His Passion and Drama for Mankind
(NASB, John. 18.1-40). FULL TEXT

18 When Jesus had spoken these words, He went forth with His disciples over the [a]ravine of the Kidron, where there was a garden, in which He entered [b]with His disciples. 2 Now Judas also, who was [c]betraying Him, knew the place, for Jesus had often met there with His disciples. 3 Judas then, having received the Roman [d]cohort and officers from the chief priests and the Pharisees, *came there with lanterns and torches and weapons. 4 So Jesus, knowing all the things that were coming upon Him, went forth and *said to them, "Whom do you seek?"5 They answered Him, "Jesus the Nazarene." He *said to them, "I am He." And Judas also, who was betraying Him, was standing with them.6 So when He said to them, "I am He," they drew back and fell to the ground. 7 Therefore He again asked them, "Whom

do you seek?" And they said, "Jesus the Nazarene." 8 Jesus answered, "I told you that I am He; so if you seek Me, let these go their way," 9 to fulfill the word which He spoke, "Of those whom You have given Me I lost not one." 10 Simon Peter then, having a sword, drew it and struck the high priest's slave, and cut off his right ear; and the slave's name was Malchus. 11 So Jesus said to Peter, "Put the sword into the sheath; the cup which the Father has given Me, shall I not drink it?"

12 So the Roman [e]cohort and the [f]commander and the officers of the Jews, arrested Jesus and bound Him, 13 and led Him to Annas first; for he was father-in-law of Caiaphas, who was high priest that year. 14 Now Caiaphas was the one who had advised the Jews that it was expedient for one man to die on behalf of the people.

15 Simon Peter was following Jesus, and so was another disciple. Now that disciple was known to the high priest and entered with Jesus into the court of the high priest, 16 but Peter was standing at the door outside. So the other disciple, who was known to the high priest, went out and spoke to the doorkeeper, and brought Peter in. 17 Then the slave-girl who kept the door *said to Peter, "You are not also one of this man's disciples, are you?" He *said, "I am not." 18 Now the slaves and the officers were standing there, having made a charcoal fire, for it was cold and they were warming themselves; and Peter was also with them, standing and warming himself.

19 The high priest then questioned Jesus about His disciples, and about His teaching. 20 Jesus answered him, "I have spoken openly to the world; I always taught in [g]synagogues and in the temple, where all the Jews come together; and I spoke nothing in secret. 21 Why do you question Me? Question those who have heard what I spoke to them; they know what I said." 22 When He had said this, one of the officers standing nearby struck Jesus, saying, "Is that the way You answer the high priest?" 23 Jesus answered him, "If I have spoken wrongly, testify of the wrong; but if rightly, why do you strike Me?" 24 So Annas sent Him bound to Caiaphas the high priest.

25 Now Simon Peter was standing and warming himself. So they said to him, "You are not also one of His disciples, are you?" He denied it, and said, "I am not." 26 One of the slaves of the high priest, being a relative of the one whose ear Peter cut off, *said, "Did I not see you in the garden with Him?" 27 Peter then denied it again, and immediately a rooster crowed.

28 Then they *led Jesus from Caiaphas into the [h]Praetorium, and it was early; and they themselves did not enter into the [i]Praetorium so that they would not be defiled, but might eat the Passover. 29 Therefore Pilate went out to them and *said, "What accusation do you bring against this Man?" 30 They answered and said to him, "If this Man were not an evildoer, we would not have delivered Him to you." 31 So Pilate said to them, "Take Him yourselves, and judge Him according to your law." The Jews said to him, "We are not permitted to put anyone to death," 32 to fulfill the word of Jesus which He spoke, signifying by what kind of death He was about to die.

33 Therefore Pilate entered again into the Praetorium, and summoned Jesus and said to Him, "Are You the King of the Jews?" 34 Jesus answered, "Are you saying this [j]on your own initiative, or did others tell you about Me?" 35 Pilate answered, "I am not a Jew, am I? Your own nation and the chief priests delivered You to me; what have You done?" 36 Jesus answered, "My kingdom [k]is not of this world. If My kingdom were of this world, then My servants would be fighting so that I would not be handed over to the Jews; but as it is, My kingdom is not [l]of this realm." 37 Therefore Pilate said to Him, "So You are a king?" Jesus answered, "You say correctly that I am a king. For this I have been born, and for this I have come into the world, to testify to the truth. Everyone who is of the truth hears My voice." 38 Pilate *said to Him, "What is truth?"

And when he had said this, he went out again to the Jews and *said to them, "I find no guilt in Him. 39 But you have a custom that I release someone [m]for you at the Passover; do you wish then that I release [n]for you the King of the Jews?" 40 So they cried out again, saying, "Not this Man, but Barabbas." Now Barabbas was a robber.

Footnotes:
a. John 18:1
b. John 18:1
c. John 18:2
d. John 18:3
e. John 18:12
f. John 18:12
g. John 18:20
h. John 18:28
i. John 18:28
j. John 18:34
k. John 18:36
l. John 18:36
m. John 18:39
n. John 18:39

Highlight to draw the saving Grace of our Lord out, v33 the dialogue between Pilate and Jesus read all the way to v40.Again look at the dialogue in (NIV, John. 19.19). Pilate had a notice prepared and fastened to the cross. It read: JESUS OF NAZARETH. THE KING OF THE JEWS. V21 The chief priests protested to Pilate to have it removed and Pilate replied in v22" What I have written, I have written". So, my brothers and sisters in Christ, when sometimes ideas or things never work the way we anticipated it to be, walk away or leave the fight for another day, remember how Jesus must have felt on this sad day, that everything He came down to do were reduced to word of word.

5.6 At the Foot of The Cross; Mary and Others (NIV, JOHN. 19.25-29).

There are lot to be said for those our Lord called that day to the foot of the cross, when the storm of life hit, it is indeed that time we as individual really have a clue who really love or who will stick by us, it reminded me of Deon Warwick song "In good times and in bad times" can I really count on you, that is what friends are for". Our Heavenly Father picked those people that day to represent us, we have a mother-how is your relationship with your own mother? We have Mary Magdalene a young female apostle in women ministry, Mary Jesus mother, her sister a family, then Mary wife of Clopas a neighbor and John the youngest of the Apostles whom He loves due to age-youth reprsentative. The more we look at those present on the cross that day and asked the question, why did He just picked only five people, the more we understand that even though He already knew how it will end, He was still teaching us His goodness and Love which interwoven in both the First Commandment and the Second Commandment, those two greatest teaching were on the Cross with Our Lord. The essence of His passion. He emptied Himself out for us-Humility with Agape Love.

Verse 26-27 check how quickly Jesus handed His mother to John in verse 27. "And to the disciple, "Here is your mother", from that time on this disciple (John) took her into his home. Look at that, if we look closely and think what just happened-our Lord met John right there at the cross. We should pray every day to Jesus to allow us to answer our names in Heaven when the book of life is open, because that will be the essence of life-well-lived.

He gave John task to do to provide for His mother while He's gone forever from this world and the only time we will all see Jesus will be on Resurrection day. Mary's journey just started and the Lord needed a caretaker for His mother and our mother, Jesus knew the journey is not over and it can't never be over until the last triumph sound calling all angels home, those of His children that fight it out through perseverance of their faith, we have to pause each time we look at our Lord on the cross and those people present that day and ask, why these few people, He picked them for a reason, He sees our heart-out of the abundance of our heart, His miracles in all of us. Life is a battle field. (pause prayer of perseverance in our faith).

Heaven can wait Can Heaven wait? No, it cannot. This question has been posed many times to people and nobody can answer the question adequately, either we choose to ignore the question, or we really don't know what to make of it. None of us, it is a legitimate question which requires our honest answer. We know none of us can hold the Time.

Jesus is the ultimate judge and the keeper of Time. Which was the reason every chance He get to teach in the sacred Text do the peace signs to the audiences. He always asked us and trying to find out about our frame of thought/minds with His Holy City? "City of God" Before He ascended to Heaven He told His followers that He was going to prepare a place for us, and that in His father house, there are many mansions, where he is we will be also. So, we really cannot do anything about it, when the individual time comes, the person must go, in the meantime, let us do good work to secure our place in our Lord 's kingdom.

Jesus is the way, the truth and the life, whosoever believes in Him shall never perish. These are some of the excuses we imposed on ourselves to sabotage our own entry into Jesus kingdom, our jobs, the children schedules, I have no baby sitters, the excuses go on and on. Indeed, we do have the options/and freedom to follow Christ, but at the end of age, two gates will be available, one will lead to Heaven and the other to Hell which is why our Lord is calling everybody to change their ways and accept Jesus as their Lord and savior. Our relationship with God matter while we're still living. On that day O. Lord, when we finally stand before you to give an account of our lives, we hope to hear you say."Come good servant when I was hungry, thirsty, naked, homeless, ill and imprisoned, you offered your gifts of time in charity and you did it for me says the Lord. Amen.

As I minister to the sick and dying, the question that majority of the sick folks asked, is it too late to either baptized or confess certain sin which most have been keeping for many years, sometimes during visiting, patient might request for a priest or a Reverend or a Pastor depending on the individual patient church, or sometimes we call the on-call pastor in an emergency cases because of a confession before the patient goes to surgery, the hospital treat the total people as needs arises, since Jesus said none of us should be deprived of His grace.

5.7 Jesus' Warning and The Gift of Holy Spirit (NASB, John. 16.1-15)

16 "These things I have spoken to you so that you may be kept from stumbling. 2 [a]They will make you outcasts from the synagogue, but an hour is coming for everyone who kills you to think that he is offering service to God. 3 These things they will do because they have not known the Father or Me. 4 But these things I have spoken to you, so that when their hour comes, you [b]may remember that I told you of them. These things I did not say to you at the beginning, because I was with you.

c. The Holy Spirit Promised

5 "But now I am going to Him who sent Me; and none of you asks Me, 'Where are You going?' 6 But because I have said these things to you, sorrow has filled your heart. 7 But I tell you the truth, it is to your advantage that I go away; for if I do not go away, the [c]Helper will not come to you; but if I go, I will send Him to you. 8 And He, when He comes, will convict the world concerning sin and righteousness and judgment; 9 concerning sin, because they do not believe in Me; 10 and concerning righteousness, because I go to the Father and you no

longer see Me; 11 and concerning judgment, because the ruler of this world has been judged.

12 "I have many more things to say to you, but you cannot bear them now. 13 But when He, the Spirit of truth, comes, He will guide you into all the truth; for He will not speak on His own initiative, but whatever He hears, He will speak; and He will disclose to you what is to come. 14 He will glorify Me, for He will take of Mine and will disclose it to you. 15 All things that the Father has are Mine; therefore, I said that He takes of Mine and will disclose it to you.

5.8   The Holy Spirit came at Pentecost as Promised (NASB, Acts. 2. 1-11)

1 When the day of Pentecost came, they were all together in one place.

2 Suddenly a sound like the blowing of a violent wind came from heaven and filled the whole house where they were sitting.

3They saw what seemed to be tongues of fire that separated and came to rest on each of them.

4 All of them were filled with the Holy Spirit and began to speak in other tongues as the Spirit enabled them.

5Now there were staying in Jerusalem God-fearing Jews from every nation under heaven.

6 When they heard this sound, a crowd came together in bewilderment, because each one heard their own language being spoken.

7 Utterly amazed, they asked: "Aren't all these who are speaking Galileans?

8 Then how is it that each of us hears them in our native language?

9 Parthians, Medes and Elamites; residents of Mesopotamia, Judea and Cappadocia, Pontus and Asia,

10 Phrygia and Pamphylia, Egypt and the parts of Libya near Cyrene; visitors from Rome

11 (both Jews and converts to Judaism); Cretans and Arabs—we hear them declaring the wonders of God in our own tongues!"

The Pentecost reminded us in the beginning section of the story of "Babel" here our Lord fulfilled His promises to the apostles that if they wait in Jerusalem for a certain day then he will send the comforter and the counselor the "Holy Spirit to them to guide and teach them new things. they did, and they got the result of empowerment. In the case of Babel, they were getting lazy and settle down prematurely when the job is not even started, so God gave them a push with languages so that they can conquer the world. God's children are all over the world, thanks to all the Christians missionaries who go to these remotest parts of the world to spread the good news of our Lord. May the good Lord protect you and bless your families that you left behind. Amen.

5.9 The Great Commission
(NASB, Matthew. 28.16-20)

16 But the eleven disciples proceeded to Galilee, to the mountain which Jesus had designated. 17 When they saw Him, they worshiped Him; but some were doubtful. 18 And Jesus came up and spoke to them, saying, "All authority has been given to Me in heaven and on earth. 19 [a]Go therefore and make disciples of all the nations, baptizing them in the name of the Father and the Son and the Holy Spirit, 20 teaching them to observe all that I commanded you; and lo, I am with you [b]always, even to the end of the age."

5.9 The Ascension of Our Lord (NIV, Luke. 24.50-53)

50 Then he led them out as far as Bethany, and, lifting his hands, he blessed them. 51 While he was blessing them, he withdrew from them and was carried up into heaven.[a] 52 And they worshiped him, and[b] returned to Jerusalem with great joy; 53 and they were continually in the temple blessing God.

The highlight of the Bible passage above suggests "To much is given much is expected. James said it better in (NKJV, James. 4.17). "So, whoever knows the right thing to do and fail to do it, for him it is sin". None of us came to be without God's hand in it,

He created us in His own image, and we existed because He wanted us to be. And (NKJV, Jeremiah. 1.5). echoed this saying "Before I formed you in the womb, I knew you; before you were born I "Sanctified "you, I ordained you a prophet to the nations. Remarkably this promises and grace were all passed down to us, the new generation of Christians, our Lord is an inclusive God, (Isaiah 49:16 NIV) See, I have engraved you on the palms of my hands; your walls are ever before me.

(NKJV, Jeremiah. 31.3). "You're precious in my eyes" Isaiah 43:4). again "Even the hairs on your head are all numbered" (NIV, Matthew. 10. 30). and "I will be a father to you (NIV, 2 Corinthians. 6.16). And "For I know the thoughts that I think toward you, says the Lord, thoughts of peace and not evil, to give you a future and a hope. v12 "Then you will call upon me and go and pray to Me, and I will "Listen to you. V13" And you will seek Me and find Me.

When you search for Me with all your heart." (NKJV, Jeremiah. 29.11-13). So we know His blessings is for everlasting from generation unto generation, why then do we ignore Him and count Him out in our life until is too late and we are searching He , the God that never left us, the reason is because our enemy do not want us to seek the true God, but through perseverance , His grace and promises remains with us through our baptism promises, what we need to do each day is to include Him in our sacred journey, sure we will have issues, delays, worries, anxieties, helplessness and hopelessness sometimes, but If we have that confidence in the Lord that this is only temporarily, we have conquer whatever the world dishes out. Our Lord will never let us down if we trust in His amazing grace.

Indeed, fallen humans cannot avoid sins because we are all by nature, but we do have that "Freedom to choose our battle". Our God giving consciousness allow that we can be sway but once we thought things through with reasons, repercussions and consequences of action, we ought to be in good term with self. (NKJV, I John. 5.9). God initiated our salvation and Jesus came to fulfil the promise for mankind. (NKJV, Jonah. 2.9).

We loved Him because He first loved us (NKJV, I John. 4.19). We seek Him then because He was the first who sought us. His Holy Spirit in us moved us to repentance of our sins, because without our faith it is impossible to please God. So everybody that comes to Jesus must believe that He exits and that He rewards those who earnestly seek Him (NIV, Hebrew. 11.6).

"God is found by those who seek Him, yet when they find Him they discover that He first sought them". (Norman 60).

The point I'm making here is that on any giving day at the hospital, visiting sick patients, the number one concerns about those who are in the hospital at that particular time is will God accept me the way I'm if I don't make it back to my family.

This is really real Stuff, where rubber meets the road, most of the patients I see in daily basis just want prayers, and some don't even want to talk anymore to healthcare professionals especially on a cancer patient's floor.

In my verbatim report I was able to report to my spiritual adviser in the spiritual care department that each day I was assigned to that floor I dread the visit, I guessed because I too I'm a human being and the pain was real, but the only thing we both have in common is the goodness and grace of our Lord to see us through, and at the end of our earthly journey we pray to end up in Jesus Heavenly home, because He told us to work hard and obtain them through supplication , worship and praise, through His mercy, so our relationship with God the Father will be second to none.

The Son and Holy Spirit should be our cup of tea, and none of us should delegate our salvation to another human being, we must do everything in our power not to abruptly remove our name from the: Book of Life" meaning the book of Jesus. So, any decision or judgement that will impede our spiritual growth in the area of sins we must pay attention to them closely. This time calls for Serenity prayer, my hospital lab jacket is full of them each visit.

CHAPTER 6:
The Four Last Thing

Jesus revealed to us that He is the "Resurrection and the life" (NIV, John. 11-25) in spite of His persistent warning for us to get it, those who profess that Jesus is Lord run the risk of rejection, the only logic thing to do is as long as the Bible teaches and individual teaching and preaching the gospel of salvation should continue and teach the truth.

Jesus said " I'm the gate. Whoever enters through me will be saved" (NIV, John. 10.9). A huge segment of Christians believe heaven exist than believe hell exist. Bible explained that hell is a real place to which the wicked/non-believers are sent after death. All of us have sinned against God (NIV, Romans. 3.23), and the just punishment for that sin is death. (NIV, Romans. 6.23).

The shifting trend in modern cultures made it impossible for some people to believe   the idea of everlasting torment and damnation, which made it hard for someone to swallow. Heaven and hell is real, some group will go to heaven, and some group will go to hell. which is why each opportunity Jesus gets while here on Earth Jesus always preach it and gave parables to carry the messages to people? We have to be honest to one another and call it like it is, some of us will experience eternal life (life spent eternal in communion with God) and others will experience eternal death/damnationn (life spent eternally rejecting God).

Our souls are immortal and will not die. At death we experience a particular judgement by Jesus for our lives spent here on earth. We will be judged on the basis of our Love of God and neighbor. Jesus explained this in parable of the final judgement (NASB, Matt. 15.31-46)

6.1 The Judgment: (NASB, Matthew. 25.31-46).

31 "But when the Son of Man comes in His glory, and all the angels with Him, then He will sit on His glorious throne. 32 All the nations will be gathered before Him; and He will separate them from one another, as the shepherd separates the sheep from the goats; 33 and He will put the sheep on His right, and the goats on the left.

34 "Then the King will say to those on His right, 'Come, you who are blessed of My Father, inherit the kingdom prepared for you from the foundation of the world. 35 For I was hungry, and you gave Me something to eat; I was thirsty, and you gave Me something to drink; I was a stranger, and you invited Me in; 36 naked, and you clothed Me; I was sick, and you visited Me; I was in prison, and you came to Me.' 37 Then the righteous will answer Him, 'Lord, when did we see You hungry, and feed You, or thirsty, and give You something to drink? 38 And when did we see You a stranger, and invite You in, or naked, and clothe You? 39 When did we see You sick, or in prison, and come to You?' 40 The King will answer and say to them, 'Truly I say to you, to the extent that you did it to one of these brothers of Mine, even the least of them, you did it to Me.'

41 "Then He will also say to those on His left, 'Depart from Me, accursed ones, into the eternal fire which has been prepared for the devil and his angels; 42 for I was hungry, and you gave Me nothing to eat; I was thirsty, and you gave Me nothing to drink; 43 I was a stranger, and you did not invite Me in; naked, and you did not clothe Me; sick, and in prison, and you did not visit Me.' 44 Then they themselves also will answer, 'Lord, when did we see You hungry, or thirsty, or a stranger, or naked, or sick, or in prison, and did not [a]take care of You?' 45 Then He will answer them, 'Truly I say to you, to the extent that you did not do it to one of the least of these, you did not do it to Me.' 46 These will go away into eternal punishment, but the righteous into eternal life."

We have two sources of problem today in our society from those in position of authority or influence in the church who do not understand human and family dynamics, in a way we might as well say it, blind leading the blind, they are good people trying to do the best they could do but fall short in the area of spirituality, this area is individuality, it is not a one size fit all.

My spiritual needs is different from my sister coming up behind me, the problems most people I encounter when I see them in the hospital during visiting hour is nobody listens to me, not the pastor not the clergy, they just lump me with the rest of the people, or when I confided with my pastors as in confession or come for counseling, my problems become an open book or a sermon on Sunday morning with the pastors, most of these pastor s are not ordained or have never gone to school to improve or acquire knowledge to serve the people God wanted them to lead, this is ironic, to think the only sermon Jesus preach the most while on earth we're sugar coating it.

He told us the truth, that Heaven and hell did existed, He created it for children of the darkness, and He gave us clues how to arrive to His kingdom, but those in authority are not sharing the full information, perhaps they fear they will lose members,

I would rather now the trip ahead of time and prepare well in advice than this trip I have no clue, but if I had done the homework, the outcome could have been in my favor.

We know that only one trial is accorded each of us. We have to prepare ourselves to meet the king while we are in good health and not wait for last minute on the death bed looking for someone to save us, Jesus has been with us and will forever be with us as the children of God acknowledge daily. So not everyone is going to Heaven, He said that but for those who does the will of His Father will end up in His kingdom.

If you have a church and they are not talking about Heaven and Hell and how to avoid the later, please you owe your soul while you can to exit that church and seek another that will validate it in the Bible those two doctrines Jesus spent each day on earth defending and which ultimately led them crucified Him. Ecclesiastes 9:5 says the living know they will die, but the dead do not know anything".

Sinner has to be punished, or God is not just. (NIV, 2 Thessalonians. 1.6). The judgment we face at death is God bringing our accounts up to date and passing sentence on our crimes against Him. What did we do. (NIV, 1 Corinthians 6.6-11); said "Do you not know that wrongdoers will not inherit the kingdom of God? Do not be deceived, neither the sexually immoral nor idolaters, nor adulterers nor men who have sex with men nor thieves nor the greedy nor drunkards nor slanderers nor swindlers will inherit the kingdom of God. And that is what some of you were.

But you were washed, you were sanctified, you were justified in the name of the Lord Jesus Christ and by the Spirit of God "The sacrifice of Jesus on the cross covers it all. The people who go to Heaven are us the sinners, who have placed their trust, faith in the Lord Jesus Christ (NIV, John. 1.12). Acts 16.31 and Romans 10.9), they recognized their deeds and humbly asked God for forgiveness. (NIV, Mark 8.34; and John 15.14). And served the Lord, answered the call of the table of the Lamb. They did not cover the sins but allowed God to transform them to another level with their gifts of "Time".

Jesus is the resurrection. He holds the key to death. Death is not the end for all the Christians who put their trust in the Lord. In (NIV, John. 20.17), after the resurrection of our Lord in the tomb, Mary could not hold on to Jesus because He had not yet gone to Heaven to His Father and our Father the Almighty God. We Christians have to put our inductive reasoning and logic to read the Bible passages, to have meaning for us, each Sunday after church when you get home, force yourself to go over the reading for the day and ask simple question like, what is the passage trying to tell me personally, aside the pastors own version.

I tell you our pastors will not be with us that day, this is real as it gets and the moment we all buckle up, roll up our sleeves and let Jesus in out boat, the better we will be, nobody can delegate this or lawyer-up on this event, Me and you we either have it or not, I wish everybody in the Lord safe trip to Heaven." Our ultimate permanent home" Amen.

6.2 The Body and the Soul

1. Soul-We are created above the animals in that we have a rational soul which means we know God. Have the freedom and will to love or reject God.

This ability to know and love God and the freedom to choose to serve Him or not, makes us responsible for our thoughts, action Body- Our body and soul makes up a whole person. Therefore, on the day of final judgment, those who have lived a life of God will receive their resurrected and glorified body.

After the final judgment the saints will united totally to God, completely as a whole person, this has been prefigured by Jesus Resurrection from the dead.

2. Death and judgement.

a. Life in eternity depends on the state of the soul at the moment of death

b. At the moment of death, the soul is separated from the body

c. The Christian who has lived loving and neighbor, there is no fear of death. Death is merely a doorway to the hope of eternal life.

6.2 b. Judgement

There are 2 judgements recorded in the Bible

1. Particular Judgment:

After death the soul is instantaneously judged on how he or she has lived their life here on earth.

At this moment, the soul receives it's just and eternal reward.

a. either to enter into Heaven immediately or through temporary purification

b. Or to enter into immediate and everlasting damnation

6.3 The Last Judgement. CCC1038-1041)

This is the last judgment for all mankind from throughout all time. When Christ return in glory. The final resurrection is preceded by the resurrection of the dead.

we shall know the ultimate effects of our sins on human history, as well as the effects of our love of God and neighbor on human history too.

At the last judgment, our soul will be united with our body's complete eternal blessedness or complete damnation.

The Angel said, "Men of Galilee, why do you stand looking into heaven? This Jesus, who was taken up from you into heaven, will come in the same way as you saw him go into heaven."(ESV, Act 1.11),

2.   Heaven (: CCC1023-1029)

A.Immediate: those who die in God's grace and are perfectly purified live forever with Christ.

B. Heaven is complete union with God.

3. Through Purification. Purgatory, as Christians we leave no stone untouched. (CCC1030-1032);

a. Those who die in God grace and friendship, but die with sins, are assured eternal life, but purification first, We as Christians must try and revealed everything that pertain to our salvation, it's not our place to pass judgement whether an event or any deeds will pass the recommended standard of our Lord Jesus Christ, but we should allow others to make that determination of revealed mysteries of our Lord.

b. God cannot be united with sinners (which are the rejection of God)-Scripture speaks of purifying fire that souls undergo that they may be purified from their sins to achieve the holiness necessary to enter the joy of heaven.

c. Prayers of relatives and friends on earth can assist those in purgatory-communion of saints. We Christians of all faith agreed just as we have many living saints in our midst through their work of Mercy, we also have saints who have already died in the service of our Lord, we must have recognized them as well. They see what we don't see and continue to cheer us up for the service of our Lord. We need their prayers for perseverance of our salvation until we see Jesus face to face. From conception to natural death, we need people of God to pray for us and with us.

Hell
1. No one goes to hell by God's choice
2. Hell is a perpetual state of rejection of God

6.4 The Reality of Death, Judgement, Heaven and Hell

"And I saw the dead, great and small, standing before the throne, and books were opened. Another book was opened, which is the book of life. The dead were judged according to what they had done as recorded in the books". (ESV, Revelation. 20.12).

We will all be judged, regardless of our denominations, political affiliates, all nations on Earth will be judged by Jesus Christ, because, He said nobody come to God without passing through Him. Your pastors will go through the judgement seat of God, mine too, every single one of us, no exception in the eyes of the Lord, we have all sinned and come short of His glory, but through His grace we have been saved, our faith and deeds will determine the next levels , whether will go to Heaven with Him or to the r other side, we still have the chance to safe our souls from destruction and the pain of hell. Calling all Christians to repent their sins and come to Jesus. Let review what Jesus told Nicodemus.

6.5 Jesus and Nicodemus a call to repentance
(NASB, John. 3. 1-21)

3 Now there was a man of the Pharisees, named Nicodemus, a ruler of the Jews; 2 this man came to Jesus by night and said to Him, "Rabbi, we know that You have come from God as a teacher; for no one can do these [a]signs that You do unless God is with him." 3 Jesus answered and said to him, "Truly, truly, I say to you, unless one is born [b]again he cannot see the kingdom of God."

4 Nicodemus *said to Him, "How can a man be born when he is old? He cannot enter a second time into his mother's womb and be born, can he?" 5 Jesus answered, "Truly, truly, I say to you, unless one is born of water and the Spirit he cannot enter into the kingdom of God. 6 That which is born of the flesh is flesh, and that which is born of the Spirit is spirit. 7 Do not be amazed that I said to you, 'You must be born [c]again.' 8 The wind blows where it wishes and you hear the sound of it, but do not know where it comes from and where it is going; so is everyone who is born of the Spirit."

9 Nicodemus said to Him, "How can these things be?" 10 Jesus answered and said to him, "Are you the teacher of Israel and do not understand these things? 11 Truly, truly, I say to you, we speak of what we know and testify of what we have seen, and you do not accept our testimony. 12 If I told you earthly things and you do not believe; how will you believe if I tell you heavenly things? 13 No one has ascended into heaven, but He who descended from heaven: the Son of Man. 14 As Moses lifted up the serpent in the wilderness, even so must the Son of Man be lifted up;15 so that whoever [d]believes will in Him have eternal life.

16 "For God so loved the world, that He gave His [e]only begotten Son, that whoever believes in Him shall not perish, but have eternal life.17 For God did not send the Son into the world to judge the

world, but that the world might be saved through Him. 18 He who believes in Him is not judged; he who does not believe has been judged already, because he has not believed in the name of the [f] only begotten Son of God.19 This is the judgment, that the Light has come into the world, and men loved the darkness rather than the Light, for their deeds were evil. 20 For everyone who does evil hates the Light and does not come to the Light for fear that his deeds will be exposed. 21 But he who practices the truth comes to the Light, so that his deeds may be manifested as having been wrought in God."

Footnotes:
a. John 3:2
b. John 3:3
c. John 3:7
d. John 3:15
e. John 3:16
f. John 3:18

6.6 The Discussion:

Jesus told Nicodemus that he must repent, change his way and be baptized with water and Holy Spirit, the Holy Spirit through our Lord Jesus by His Sanctifying grace we were all healed. We remembered the Pentecost Sunday, how He impacted His Holy Spirit to all His Apostles, even those who were not there that day, He came for them later and they received His Holy Spirit. Jesus already told us that, for some rich folks and influential people receiving the gospel would be too much, because they will not want to part with friends and their lifestyles of rich and famous, and He told us, those who do not want to associate themselves with Him, He too will reject them. He said again in their synagogues He came for those who are sick and in need of a healer. Our Lord is God of inclusion, He love us very much.

We have to believe and through faith all things are possible for children of God. The soul upon death will either go to God the giver of Life or to the opposing enemy, once life ceases, the deceased person has no control of where the soul goes, which is why while living to do the work of our Lord, repent of our sins, believe and have faith, that our Lord's grace will be sufficient to get us home to His paradise- "City of God". Amen

CHAPTER 7:
Background Mission and Ministry Pastoral Care of The Sick.

The Sermon on the Mount to me clearly indicated what all Christians should practice. Today Christians with my observation, are timid, nobody wants to correct anybody for fair that they will label them, we have become one size fits all, we have become "Whatever" we don't want to offend anyone if what we saw or perceive in our heart did not add up to realistic expectation of that individual, we remain silence. The message and teachings of Jesus Christ has become "Water Down" doctrine a prosperity doctrine, by no means there is nothing wrong in preaching self-sufficient and accumulation of wealth, but He also warned us not to overproduce which can lead to greed and lawlessness.

Everybody wants to live better and well but if all you hear is how to make money and keeping it and cheat others out of their well earn money is just as bad as killing someone, because the pain is real. Jesus made it clear that ultimate judgement will take place, and also made it abundantly clear that those who truly believe in Him will be avoided this judgement because their sins have already been forgiven" I know my sheep, and my sheep knows me. I call them they come and follow me (NIV, John. 10. 9, 14), Again in (NIV, John 3.18-21), re-emphasized the saving grace of our Lord. His blessed assurance and promises Divine.

We have to sober up and ask Him to give us His grace while we still can do so, because after death all deeds are brought into judgment. All man's effort are his mouth, yet his appetite is never satisfied NIV, (Ecclesiastes 6:7).

Footnotes:
a. John 10: 9
b. Ecclesiastes 6:7
c. John 10:14

41 For truly, I say to you, whoever gives you a cup of water to drink because you belong to Christ will by no means lose his reward.

My project is not to side which side is wrong or on the point, my project has really moved from pulpit to healthcare setting, the people I visit really don't have time to be analyzing and side which side makes oral or academic argument. My area of specialization is nursing and now spirituality. Majority of the people I see in any given day are people who are seriously sick and confided with me their deepest and spiritual , emotional helplessness, these people worry with anxieties about their relationship with God, how and what they can do to reconnect back to Him.

There is fear, hopelessness, helplessness, fear of abandonment from loved ones, we have to note that, they are sick now, some of them have moved-in with other family members, they are vulnerable and they seek solace with God, and I know our Lord is a forgiving God, Most of my visit is to just Listen to what they have to say, non-judgmental approach with open arms-offers the presence of the Lord in a caring capacity.

I assist them with simple request, for example, some patients could request for a priest if they're Catholics, some request for a pastor/reverend if they Baptist, Lutheran and some request for Elders depending on their church affiliates, some request for Rabbi and some Imam, since the hospital is an ecumenical approach to spiritual care, so our roles is multi-facet meaning in the hospital we serve all denominations.

We provided a lot of Bibles, prayer cards, religious information and we offer baptism/assist those pastors in that area. So we never judge our brothers and sisters, since the ultimate goal is to answer their questions with the best of our abilities and we make referral within the spiritual care department to appropriate church affiliates within the hospital.

The question here worth noticing is that most people I encounter really are running on empty, there are lot of spiritual emptiness , our Lord told us to " seek first the things that are above then everything will be added, with observation these are not the case, people are really busy trying to hit it big or building wealth, and forget the most critical component "Eternity" and souls were deprived of God's grace and Heavenly nourishment, we are all guilty of that. But it is not too late, we can always come to Jesus with contrite heart and our Lord will open His arms to forgive and bless us.

7.1 Running on Empty Footprint in the Sand

One night a man had a dream. He dreamt he was walking along the beach with the Lord. Across the sky flashed scenes from his life. For each scene, he noticed two sets of footprints in the sand, one belonging to him, and the other to the Lord. When the last scene of his life flashed before him, he looked back at the footprints in the sand, he noticed that many times along the path of his life there was only one set of footprints. He also noticed that it happened at the very lowest and saddest times in his life.

This really bothered him, and he questioned the Lord about it. "LORD, you said that once I decided to follow you, you will walk with me all the way. But I have noticed that during the most troublesome times in my life, there is only one set of footprints. I don't understand why when I needed you the most you would leave me. The LORD replied, "My precious, precious child, I love you and I would never leave you. During your times of trial and suffering, when you see only one set of footprints, it was then that I carried you".

Life is a journey, with every twist and turns, we need Jesus to be able to navigate and not get loss or distracted. We are all in exile, and it will take divine intervention to lead us back to Jesus, our enemies don't want us to reconnect or united with Him, that is why prayers are effective.

My project is about a big question and answer of, Heaven can wait, Can Heaven wait? The moment our forefather Adam and evil sinned at the beautiful Garden" that our God provided them, all grace was lost forever, and it will take another covenant to correct it. My project will explore the beginning of their journey, the coming of Jesus Christ to Earth to save mankind from their sins, and some of the obstacles and challenging we human are facing in any given day and how we became overcomers through God's grace.

The Evangelist Billy Graham said at the last crusade in Ottawa, "We don't know when the end of the world will be, but the end of the world for us is the day we die. "Of course, for that individual soul, all work on Earth is completed, Jesus call the Angel Home.

The individual and His Guardian Angel instantaneously with the Lord, only our Angel knows how to get to Heaven, face it, this is beyond our imagination or navigation, because at this realm –meaning in spiritual realm only the Angel of the LORD can transfer soul one person at a time, and still be a ministering spirit as well.

We will not know or feel l a thing, but Jesus just begins His saving grace on our behalf, but while alive we need to make our needs know to God that we belong to Him and not our adversary, once death take place all works seize. Pause and praise our Lord here. The Lord Prayer adds psalm 23 will be the most effective one here, and (John 10: 9, 14). As a nurse in ICU for twenty years and I have witnessed many patients die in my arms, no families at bedside for some of them, no amount of medication to revived them, you just have to give Honor and respect to God Almighty for the Gift of Lives, we have to be serious about the last four things.

The non-chalant attitude about Heaven and Hell in this modern time is very serious, we blame each other for failure to thrive, to get ahead in life, blame others for our own safety and "Eternity", mark you some of these patients I see in hospital majority of the time are in median age of 66. And the oldest I encountered was 98 years old. So, we have time to walk with Jesus, so repent and be saved.

Until we take this seriously our Lord said this in the Sacred Text that we never search for Him, here are two passages to remind us the goodness of our Lord. (Job 36: 12, ESV). v12 " But if they do not listen, they perish by the sword and die without knowledge". Again in (Hosea 4:6, NIV). "My people are destroyed from lack of knowledge. "Because you have rejected knowledge, I also reject you as my priest; because you have ignored the law of your God, I also will ignore your children". So, we have to listen to God's word and not take Him for granted. If we truly Love the Lord, we will do as He told us what to do.

FIGURE 1: YOUNG CHILDREN AND OLDER PEOPLE AS A PERCENTAGE OF THE GLOBAL POPULATION: 1950-2050[1]

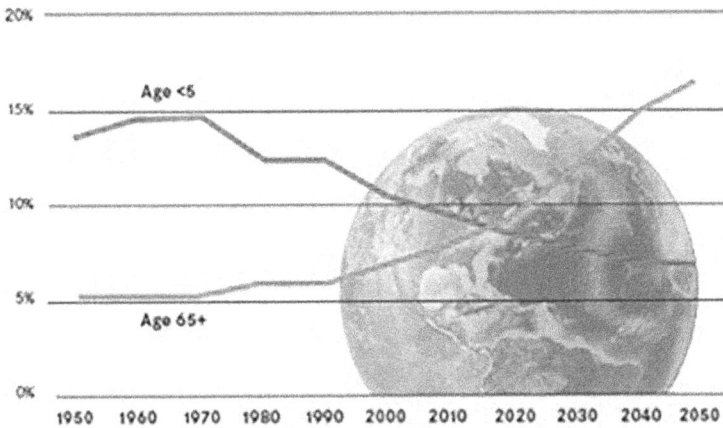

Source: *World Population Prospects: The 2010 Revision*, United Nations.
Adapted from *Global Health & Aging*, World Health Organization, 2011.

Figure 1

7.2 Aging Population and Growth

According to Health and Aging report presented by the World Health Organization (WHO), "The number of people aged 65 or older is projected to grow from an estimated 524 million in 2010 to nearly 1.5 billion in 2050, with most of the increase in developing countries." In addition, by 2050, the number of people 65 years or older is expected to significantly outnumber children younger than 5 years of age (see figure 1).

WHO attributes the elderly population's rapid size increase to a change in the leading cause of death, from infections to chronic non -communicable diseases—which increased life expectancy.1 These chronic conditions may include hypertension, high cholesterol, arthritis, diabetes, heart disease, cancer, dementia, and congestive heart failure. Heart disease, stroke, and cancer have been the leading chronic conditions that have had the greatest impact on the aging population, especially in high-income countries.1 In addition, the incidences of obesity and falls are increasing.

this leads to the question: what are the implications of the aging population on health care? We have all heard the term "baby boomer." According to the Office of Disease Prevention and Health Promotion, the first Baby Boomers (those born between 1946 and 1964) turned 65 in 2011 By 2030, it is projected that more than 60% of this generation will be managing more than one chronic condition.

Managing these chronic conditions, along with a patient's level of disability, will increase the financial demands on our health care system.3 The cost increases with the number of chronic conditions being treated, taking into account the expected twice as many hospital admissions and physician visits for Baby Boomers by 2030.

According to the WHO report, some believe that as life expectancy increases, the prevalence of disability will decrease because the progress we make in medicine will slow disease progression from chronic disease to disability. As a result, there will be a decrease in severe disability, but there will be increases in milder chronic diseases.1 other researchers, however, believe that as life expectancy increases, the prevalence of disability will increase.

There are certain health conditions that are expected to be a challenge to our health care system with the increasing aging population. These conditions include cancer, dementia, and increase in the number of falls, obesity, and diabetes.

We have to talk about health and end of life crisis, some culture are not really naive as we are in America. Some culture gets it and it never define them but embrace it that it's part of life and reference God Almighty, accept it and move on, pray that whatever they have done so far in the area of their spirituality encountering with the Lord with praise, worship and deeds that too should be sufficient for God to look kindly on their work. This is contentment.

American Evangelical leaders reflected on whether the United States is a Christian nation, the ironic thing happened 68% said it is not in the 2012 survey. Another responses suggested that "perhaps the United States was a Christian nation before, but it is no longer, Others rejected the idea of a nation can be "Christian altogether" and the most profound thing about the survey was that, most of the people survey, 32% said they thought United States was founded on Christian principles, they voted that way but were never a follower of any religion.

Let's face it, there is Heaven and there is Hell. One group will go to Heaven the other group will go to Hell that is the reality of the journey. We pray each day that the joy of our Lord be our strength. Jesus said yet again in (NASB, John. 14. 1-9). V6. Jesus said "Iam the way and the truth and the life. No one comes to the Father except through me".

Christians are the largest religious group in 2015

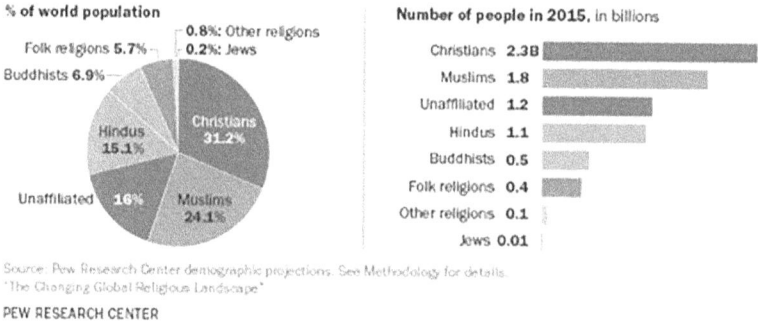

% of world population

- 0.8%: Other religions
- 0.2%: Jews
- Folk religions 5.7%
- Buddhists 6.9%
- Hindus 15.1%
- Christians 31.2%
- Unaffiliated 16%
- Muslims 24.1%

Number of people in 2015, in billions

- Christians 2.3B
- Muslims 1.8
- Unaffiliated 1.2
- Hindus 1.1
- Buddhists 0.5
- Folk religions 0.4
- Other religions 0.1
- Jews 0.01

Source: Pew Research Center demographic projections. See Methodology for details. "The Changing Global Religious Landscape"

PEW RESEARCH CENTER

Figure 2

7.3 The World Largest Religious Group

Please look at the above (figure 2). Christians remained the largest religious group in the world in 2015, making up nearly a third (31%) of Earth's 7.3 billion people, according to a new Pew Research Center demographic analysis. But the report also shows that the number of Christians in what many consider the religion's heartland, the continent of Europe, is in decline.

Globally, Muslims make up the second largest religious group, with 1.8 billion people, or 24% of the world's population, followed by religious "none's" (16%), Hindus (15%) and Buddhists (7%). Adherents of folk religions, Jews and members of other religions make up smaller shares of population.

The Christian faith inspires people to grow as followers of Jesus Christ (discipleship) and to use the gifts and talents that God has entrusted to them in His service and for His glory (Ministry). Many of our brothers and sisters want to learn more about their Christian faith and live a productive and enriching lives, others are really struggling to find the right vocations or the right churches, but like anything else ask God to show you the path to take, and He will direct you to the right churches, you might has to travel a little bit away from your comfort Zone, but just have an open mind, let His grace direct you. Our God is God of Love.

We believe each of us has an important contribution to make to any church family, and to a wider community, If God is calling you to a ministry and you have to get extra training in other to be effective member of that community, please go for it and honor God.

The point I'm trying to make is that, most of us have already gotten our assignment to assist/volunteers those time, but due to distraction in our daily lives we ignored the calling, we procrastinate, we're looking for the "Job" in fact we have already find the job, if only we could be still and hear the "gentleness of our Lord" in all nature around us.

We are one big family in Christ, and family helps to build the kingdom of God on Earth; through service to our communities. I entered one-year training as a pastoral care assistant in the Spring of 2013; the program started January 22, 2013 and lasted December 15, 2013; It was a year program at the Chaplaincy Corps Division in my Home state, it meant I have to give up my Saturdays from 9am to 1pm each weekend. Looking back, it was the best investment I ever invested-meaning the gift of "Time" to other people.

Your families and mine are not different, the only difference is how we learnt how to cope with the stressors of lives and rise up and deal with them that will determine how long we're going to stay in the" rough". So, we're going through roughness now this moment, but this too shall pass. Jesus went through humiliation, betrayal, loss of His life to save us. We have to pick ourselves up and let God handle the problems for us. Jesus said don't worry about tomorrow, God is already there, in Jeremiah 29:11 NIV. "For I know the plans I have for you" declares the Lord, "plans to prosper you and not to harm you, plan to give you hope and a future." And the second promise in Proverbs 3:5;

"Trust in the Lord with all your heart".

My program in the hospital is an "Ecumenical" according to Merriam-Webster dictionary definition, is to promote or tending toward worldwide unity or cooperation within the body of Christ.

The primary mission of the chaplaincy services within the hospital that I'm affiliated is to announce the good news. The message of our Lord Jesus Christ to share them with joy, encouraging one another, that just because this time around sickness or disease came knocking that should not steal the joy of the Lord from them, announcing the teaching, preaching and sharing the saving grace of our Lord to my brothers and sisters at bedside has always been joy for me.

My primary focus at the bedside is to bring Jesus to them. The visit is spiritual in nature, and it can quickly accelerates into both social and spiritual depending on how the recipient-meaning the patient wants to make it to be, all chaplains/pastoral assistants come with open arms, to celebrate each other and our God, we listen, we cry together, perhaps some of them are going for their test or procedure in the morning, depending on what's happening that day to our sisters/brothers in Christ, we provide spiritual materials, supports, we provide bibliotherapy, prayers is the most requested component with communion on a daily basis or weekly basis, or in extremely cases family might request a clergy, a rabbi, Imam, or a pastor depending on the events in the lives of these wonderful families we serve, in an active dying patients, some family wanted their loved one to die while a chaplain or a pastors is in attending for his/her last right, for the deceased one. Whichever step the family takes, this is a family right and we in spiritual care department respect and honor the deceased person wishes

7.4 What is Spiritual Care?

It is defined as the provision of interventions in the domain of spirituality and has long been the focus of hospital chaplains.

Spiritual care also has been accepted as a legitimate focus of nursing practice. The North American Nursing Diagnoses Association has two accepted nursing diagnoses for spirituality: 1. Spiritual distress and 2. Readiness for enhanced spiritual well-being (CCN 8/2006).

When your patients or family members experience spiritual distress the nurse or MD will make a referral, if the patient did not check religion affiliation on the admission information packets. Spiritual distress is a disruption in one's belief or values system, and this may or may not be grounded in religious belief or practice. Such distress manifests itself both emotionally and physically, from rejection of care to chronic insomnia.

b. The following symptoms indicate Spiritual distress.

1. Verbal questioning of meaning of life and purpose of illness
2. Questioning of one's belief system
3. Withdrawal from, or loss of, relationship
4. Expressions of anxiety, anger and /or depression

c. These events can trigger spiritual distress.

1. First admission to the hospital
2. A terminal diagnosis
3. Suicidal thoughts
4. Loss of employment
5. Divorce
6. Death in the family.

Professional Healthcare Chaplains are trained to help patients and their families in spiritual distress to express pain, and work towards healing, answer questions and provide feedback.

As you go further into this persuasive report, "Heaven can wait;

Can Heaven wait? you will see that God is good all the time, and all the time, God is good. Service at bedside is also a mission work with primary focus on mercy-work, we are all missionary by God's divine nature in us, to serve one another, we will look at the "greatest commandments" Jesus modified for us, and we will find our own struggles in them, and knowing none of us is better than the next brother or sister behind us or in front of us, due to our common "Bond". In Ecclesiastes 9:3-6; NIV

7.5 Men are in the Hand of God
(NASB, Ecclesiastes. 9. 1-6)

9 For I have taken all this to my heart and explain [a]it that righteous men, wise men, and their deeds are in the hand of God. Man does not know whether it will be love or hatred; anything [b]awaits him.

2 It is the same for all. There is one fate for the righteous and for the wicked; for the good, for the clean and for the unclean; for the man who offers a sacrifice and for the one who does not sacrifice. As the good man is, so is the sinner; as the swearer is, so is the one who [c]is afraid to swear. 3 This is an evil in all that is done under the sun, that there is one fate for all men. Furthermore, the hearts of the sons of men are full of evil and insanity is in their hearts throughout their lives. Afterwards they go to the dead. 4 For whoever is joined with all the living, there is hope; surely a live dog is better than a dead lion. 5 For the living know they will die; but the dead do not know anything, nor have they any longer a reward, for their memory is forgotten. 6 Indeed their love, their hate and their zeal have already perished, and they will no longer have a share in all that is done under the sun.

7.6 Companion on The Journey

During our commissioning day in January 2016 ceremony which we normally do every two years. The recessional hymn read "Our Lord calls us one by one through our baptismal promises to act with justice, hope, charity and love tenderly, and thus we walk by faith with humility with our God, humbly along the way, we believe in the Love of our God". It was with joy and reference to God that I made the oath to serve my brothers and sisters for another two years , when my name was called by the Bishop (Shelby) from Archdiocese Galveston-Houston, and my family and friends were there to cheer me up, nothing can compare with that joy that day, yes I have struggled to find my own foot in the universe, but at bedside each time is a joy for me, each Fridays, knowing I will never look at my watch to hurry up to some errands or do urgent work, it is a real joy for me.

I will share some information, triumphs and sadness report I witnessed as a nurse at bedside, and as a pastoral/hospital minister using my visiting log"" let your light shine before people that they will see the good things you do and praise your Father in Heaven". (NIV,Matthew. 5.16).

Footnotes:
a. Ecclesiastes 9:1
b. Ecclesiastes 9: 1
c. Matthew 5:6

This short passage is just to remind each other's that Jesus Himself laid the plan of life for us, that we must follow Him and not be persuaded with erroneous opinion or confusion, we must test everything and then arrive to a valid conclusion, by allowing them to see and made reference to Old Testament and His sovereignty was once again validated, whether the apostle believed or not what Jesus just laid out for them, to me this is irrelevant, at least He said it and therefore we know He did not hide anything from us.

We must try and make effort on our part to pick-up our own crosses and follow Jesus. What does following Jesus entails? It means deny self, the opposite of being selfish, putting end to being center of our universe all the times, learn to breathe once in a while, put goals, ambitious, and plan that we form will not be for our own purpose. "Jesus Cross" was an instrument of death. There is no half-done job or half way through. It means totally surrender to the Will of God. He emptied Himself out for us-His Passion was us.

The question we must ask ourselves then will be, "Heaven can wait; can Heaven wait? The question then become simply "ETERNITY" is at stake, after so many years on this planet, with struggling and smiling, trying to make ends meet, and we all did it with joy of the Lord in us, can we then lose the best gift ever promised to a faithful servant, can we then tell God that we goofed off.

Tell God someone made us lose it, or can we then tell God, I forget about it, knowing that on that judgement day, no lawyers will come with us, no wives or husbands can be with us, knowing that each judgement seat is only one person at a time. Jesus constantly reminded us to work smart.

27 Do not labor for the food which perishes, but for the food which endures to everlasting life, which the Son of Man will give you, because God the Father has set His seal on Him."

28 Then they said to Him, "What shall we do, that we may work the works of God?"

29 Jesus answered and said to them, "This is the work of God that you believe in Him whom He sent."

30 Therefore they said to Him, "What sign will You perform then, that we may see it and believe You? What work will You do? 31 Our fathers ate the manna in the desert; as it is written, 'He gave them bread from heaven to eat.'"

32 Then Jesus said to them, "Most assuredly, I say to you, Moses did not give you the bread from heaven, but My Father gives you the true bread from heaven. 33 For the bread of God is He who comes down from heaven and gives life to the world."

34 Then they said to Him, "Lord, give us this bread always."

35 And Jesus said to them, "I am the bread of life. He who comes to Me shall never hunger, and he who believes in Me shall never thirst. 36 But I said to you that you have seen Me and yet do not believe. 37 All that the Father gives Me will come to Me, and the one who comes to Me I will by no means cast out. 38 For I have come down from heaven, not to do My own will, but the will of Him who sent Me. 39 This is the will of the Father who sent Me, that of all He has given Me I should lose nothing but should raise it up at the last day. 40 And this is the will of Him who sent Me, that everyone who sees the Son and believes in Him may have everlasting life; and I will raise him up at the last day." (NKJV, John. 6.27-40,).

36 For what does it profit a man to gain the whole world and forfeit his soul? 37 For what can a man give in return for his soul? 38 For whoever is ashamed of me and of my words in this adulterous and sinful generation, of him will the Son of Man also be ashamed when he comes in the glory of his Father with the Holy Angel. (ESV, Mark. 8.36-38).

7.7 Mission and Ministry
The Biopsychosocial Model of Patient Care

According to this model every single person has a spiritual history. For many people, it unfolds within the context of an explicit religion tradition, but regardless how it enfolds, this spiritual history helps to shape who each patient is as a whole.

So, when life threatening illness strikes, it strikes each person in his or her totality (Ramsey 1970). This totally includes not simply the biological, psychological and social aspects of human person as well (Engel 1992), but also the spiritual aspects of the whole person as well (King 2000, McKee and Chappell 1992).

To fully get the information right, The biopsychosocial-spiritual model is not a "dualism" in which a "soul" accidently inhabits a body, but in this model, the biological, psychological, the social, and the spiritual are one distinct dimension of a person, and no one aspect can be disengaged from the whole,

Each aspect can be affected differently by a person's history and illness, and each aspect can interact and affect other aspect of the person. Some of the worries patients experienced and shared with the nurses during admission questionnaires are. 1.) fear of unknown, 2.) hopelessness, 3.) helplessness, 4.) fear of abandonment, 5). fear of death, 6.) and fear of financial insecurity.

Whereas in holistic approach to healing means that the correction of the physiological disturbances and the restoration of the milieu interior is only the beginning of the task. Holistic healing at such requires attention to the psychological, social and spiritual disturbances as well.

In short besides the milieu interior, there is also a milieu divin, Simply meant at the end of life, when the milieu interior can no longer be restored, healing is still possible, and the healing professions still have a role. Spiritual issues arise naturally in the dying process.

No matter what the patient's spiritual history, dying raises for the patient questions about the value and meaning of his or her life, suffering, and death. Also question of value are often submerge under the term, "Dignity" again question of value are under the word, "Hope" also questions of meaning are often under reported or expressed in the need for "Forgiveness" At this phase in dying process, most patients or families request "Anointing of the sick from the pastors of different faith, and sometimes families requested   private rooms for prayer vigil" and the spiritual care department provide accommodation for families requests, some families here request pastor at bedside during active dying process, the scene is very serene and sadness.

To die believing that one's life and death have been of no value is the ultimate indignity. To die believing that there is no meaning to life, suffering, or death is pretty sad.

To die alone and unforgiven is utter alienation. For the clinician to ignore these questions at the time of greatest intensity may be to abandon the patient in the hour of greatest need.

7.8 Spiritual and Religious Coping Support

Religious coping refers to how one's spiritual or religious belief, attitudes, and practices affect one's reaction to stressful life events. The most effective tools out there that measure this are RCOPE (Pargament, Koenig, and Perez 2000) and the INSPIRIT (Vandecreek, Ayres, and Bassham 1995).

The former is more general spiritual coping. it seems very relevant to the care of the dying to assess what sort of inner resources the patient has for dealing with the stress of terminal illness, this instruments measure both positive (acceptance or peace) and negative for examples, are excessive guilt or anger. On the other hand, religious coping mechanism to us as measure of religiosity might or might not be associated with a person's religious coping style. Each person is different.

Religious coping measures the internal resources and reactions. Religious support measures the resources and reaction of the religious community that can be measured on behalf of a patient. It can be considered a subset of social support (Krause 1999). However, there are no validated instruments to measure this critical component. Like I said, in a clinical setting for example in the hospital, family dynamics dictate how the care will go forward, some families want all available whatever the medicals call for, while other families want options of how to proceed with End-of-life-crises in front of them.

As Christians we are called to live soberly in doing the work of our Lord, whether we play or at work, we must do things to honor God and each other. If we fear God and have His wisdom and understanding things we make sense to us in real lives. here are three questions that relate to our everyday struggling and jostle. 1).

If you are sick from your million-dollar job right know, how many people from your office will come to your bedside for a visit? 2). How vulnerable are you after two weeks or three weeks away from your job? 3). Do you think after so many weeks out sick, the job will still be there when you go back? 4) What keep you going every day? Your families, your jobs, or combination of both?

Well if you answer two out of four, you're running on empty in the area of spiritual soundness. This is not a judgement roll call, but to have an awareness of what really matter in our journey of faith. Do you know scripture reveals that some Christians will actually forfeit their rewards because of unrepentance sins, or failure to obey God? (NIV, Thessalonians. 4.13-18). (NIV, 1 Corinthians. 15.51-52). (NIV, Romans. 14.10-13). And (NIV, 2 Corinthians. 5.9-11 NIV). Also, some will even experience a sense of shame at the judgement commencement day. (NIV, 2 John. 8. 1). So if we know all these, does the possibility of losing your well earn reward in front of Jesus motivate you to do better or does it scare you?

As a witness at bedside, I see how families struggled to wrestle with that one thing at the end-of life-crisis. Most families wish their mothers or fathers reconciled that faith   before this crisis, and the request know for prayers become an intercessory one from a child either to a father or to a mother.

This is really profound and serious undertaking, patients and family sometimes will request prayer vigil for an active dying family member, yes family can request prayer for their loved ones, this is well document in the Holy Bible Abraham prayed for Lot his nephew. I guess what I am trying to say, is we should always put our Lord ahead of everything we do, to prevent us having panic intrusiveness.

This is not a joke folks, the scripture informed us that after death, we will be of trammels of the body, thus we see clearly, and we can see that God is supreme and infinite good. One thing certain after death, we cannot do things over "life journey is accounted for" our responsibility and accountability is strictly enforced by Divine Majesty. If sins then cause you to forgo eternity, remember those words. "We do have free will you know".

Saint Bernard wrote. "The most terrible penalty of the damned is being shut out forever from blissful and joyous contemplation of the blessed Trinity. Father, Son and Holy Spirit.

In Heaven, there are no religious affiliation, God already knows how you lead your lives, so we might as well cut this out, whether you are a Baptist, Methodist, evangelical, protestant, Seven-day Adventist, Apostolic church, Lutheran, Rabbi or Muslim, Jesus already knew, so are we Christians or not, do we do His Holy will, can we bi-pass the hot seat and go straight to Heaven. The answer is "No". The wages of sin is death, but the true grace of our Lord is eternal life.

Jesus came to Earth to save us from hell, but we must do our part to repay the debt we owe Him. He died on the cross for us and we must die too on the cross through this suffering and be with Him in His Heavenly Kingdom". we have to eat the bread and drink the cup and proclaim His death until He comes again. Many religious affiliates have ways of bringing or sharing this to their congregation, the last supper was the last act of our Lord in which, He invited the twelve first, and told them to do this in remembrance of Him, so they passed this on to us.

The hospital ministry I'm affiliated with is "Interfaith Mission"- Ecumenical"the communion is celebrated according to patient-specific, meaning since we have many church organizations within the hospital wall . some patients want communion daily, some weekly, and some once a month, and in fact for hospital patients, we cater for the total person, spirituality is determined by patients calling the shot out of respect for individuals. The hospital have one "Tabernacle "and each morning or each shift the pastoral assistants or chaplains can bring communion to the hospital patients as they needed it, we have all been trained as Holy communion servers according to our churches affiliations, but in an emergency cases we sometimes cross –over during extreme cases to assist any pastors on-call duty.

The story of these people was Jesus' story, He commissioned us to help one another through the good times and bad times. Each of us is given a gift, our names have already written in the book of life, all living and the deceased, so we cannot take our names off unless we chose to ignore the fact that Heaven Can Wait; Can Heaven Wait? Indeed not, as you go over these real encounters with people of God during my visit for the past five years, these were just small portion of my log (See table V). Please pray for those who are in the hospital currently and have nobody to visit or have no families to call them.

7.9 PCM VISITORS LOGSHEETS

Date	Patient Names	Prayer request, Bible communion, annointing of the sick, baptism information, etc	Comments, updates and report for the visits. Name of chaplain(s) or pastoral assitants:

Table V

7.9b Mission and Ministry Hospital Visits

Hospital Visit Client Number One

Every Friday I visited the sick in the hospital, I do this on my off day from work. My assigned floor today was floor 12th to 16th floors with Holy communion, on my communion list I had only three patients to see. It was a beautiful day.

The nation just celebrated the "Thanksgiving" a day earlier, the festive mood still in the air, for examples many homes still have the left-over turkey trimmings, and many guests have not left town. The atmosphere was a pleasant one. The hospital lobby when I got there was serene, no noise, the hallway all quiet, few visitors passed me by, unlike when there were no holiday, the lobby areas always packed with visitors, patients and families. I proceeded to my department, picked up my assignment and off I went to the floors.

My first client was a twenty-two years old, very pleasant young man. He had requested for Communion a day before and his name was recorded for service today for 1pm.

I introduced myself, and He introduced himself, we talked, I then asked him that he ordered a communion for this hour, and he replied yes, I did, I then asked if he's ready to receive it know, the young man said: I'm ready. So, I gave the communion, we talked some more, I then asked the patient if he wanted anything from our department "Spiritual care dept.". He said next time a Bible will do. I then thanked him, and we prayed, and I left.

Hospital Visit Client Number Two

My second client was a 64 years old female with multiples diagnosis, she was able to talk, I introduced myself, and she did also. She was so happy that we have the program at this hospital, she told me her church affiliation and I told her if she ever need a pastor, we have them here in the building, that she will encounter three professionals, one will be a chaplain, a hospital ministers, and a pastoral assistants but we all work with an ordained priest/clergy, Reverends/pastors of different faith, and she can tell me everything and I will let her know if her request needed a pastor or me getting things for her, she needed not worries because we have all the pastors on speed dial., and that our department is open 24 hours/7 days a week.

The patient laughed, a bond was formed between me and her. She asked if I have a rosary with in my servant bag and how to pray it and I said of course. I then open my servant bag, I pull a rosary and how to pray it out, and gave it to her, and she was so happy and thank the department for the work of our Lord. I gave her our department card and some biblical passages prayer cards. She also received her communion that day. I thanked her, and I left.

Hospital Visit Client Number Three

My third client was on the sixteen floor, a 60-year-old man. This visit was both spiritual and social. the patient was very kind and gentle spirit, he asked a lot of question from me, which some of the questions have nothing to do with my visit, but as a trained nurse and a pastoral assistant I was able to answer the question to the best of my ability with professionalism, at the same time was able to focus on the visit without me being the topic of the visit,

I accomplished a lot from him He was from Alabama, away from home. He asked me whether I have been away from Houston, I told him no.

I then asked him if he needed anything from my department, the fact that his church was part of the team here at the hospital fascinated him. Patient requested for a prayer at the bedside and a Bible, which I provided.

He placed his hand on the surgical site on toward the abdomen, a day earlier according to him had an abdominal ventral hernia repair. The incision was still visible. Patient informed me he read all the daily inspirational for the day on his IPAD, and that he's caught up with it. for prayer request, he picked healing and trust in the Lord. For that according to healing psalm a psalm 3:3-5 was read, and he prayed for himself because I told him to since part of my job is to encourage people to pray for themselves especially those who could do so, and I helped him to close the prayer.

He was so happy that I encouraged him to say the prayer, and I gave him the department phone number in case he needed to talk to someone after office hour. We said our goodbyes with Jesus love for both of us.

Hospital Visit Client Number Four

This was my oldest patient today, she was 83-year-old male, and the youngest in the sense that, the moment I opened my mouth and said, "peace be unto this house"" my patient was just laughing and asked where do I come from? I replied, "Jesus sent me to you today". I told him, this hospital space/room is your house" because for the next x days, this is where we will find you until the doctor discharge you to go home to your family.

We developed a bond right away, she was a very pleasant elderly man, he told me all he had to go through all week in the areas of his care, and all the test.

He asked my heritage and I told him, was not it obvious, we both laughed again. He asked me to pray for him, and I told him we are doing it right know, we prayed together, he asked for department phone number and I provided it, told him if he can't sleep tonight our department is open 24/7 and someone will answer the phone and the on-call person can come to bedside to ministering, that really provided him assurance that he was not alone. We parted with good news of our Lord.

Hospital Visit Client Number Five

This patient was 62 years old male on seventeen floor, he had been in the hospital now for more than a month, and I had visited numerous time, at one visit, he coded while I was on my way to visit, so I could not see him that day. He could not talk after the code, they inserted tube feeding through his nose to feed him, iv fluid everywhere. He was a very sick man. Each visit I will talk to him and he will request prayer from the Lord. I always told him, God love His people. I always informed him that any chaplain that comes to his bedside, he should request the same prayer he asked me and to believe what he asked for from the Lord. two weeks gone by, there was no sitter by his side today. His skin color normal, but still has the 02 @ 2l/NC by his nose.

patient was feeding himself, his health had really improved.

The nurses and doctors were so impressed with him doing better and were talking about allowing him to go back to the nursing home in about three days. I gave him his communion and we prayed afterward, we both blessed one another. This was the highlight of my visit today. Prayers are our means to communicate our needs to God, He listens to our plea, and we have to do it daily or every chance we get. God is necessary, "Man has two eyes, one only sees what moves in fleeing time, the other what is eternal and divine. Our Lord word stands for ever. (NIV, Isaiah. 40.5-6)." And the glory of the Lord shall be revealed, and all flesh shall see it together, for the mouth of the Lord has spoken" A voice says, "cry And I said, "what shall I cry? All flesh is grass, and all its beauty is like the flower of the field."

Hospital Visit Client Number Six: 01/08/2016

Grace to you and peace be multiplied this was greeting s from Apostle Peter to the newly converted Christians in Galatia, Asia, Pontus and Bithynia. Peter here was encouraging them to stay tough and stand steadfast with they're newly acquired faith. Staying with our Lord is the best option we have so far. And whoever stay with Jesus shall never perish. (1 peter NKJV).

My hospital visit today was a blessing . Slowly but surely the new year rolled in without a hitch. For me it was a new beginning, old self out, and new journey forward, 2016 came with a promising upward bound with grace and blessing from God Almighty.

Onward Christians solders matching to war with the banner of our Lord Jesus going before us. I visited St. Luke's today, 01/08/2016.

Hospital Visit Client Number Seven

My patient today was a 70-year-old, As usual I entered his room, introduced myself, he was eager to see me. Prior to my visit, from our department, I checked the log to see what the client needed, so that I can bring those items with me to the floor; For this patient, he had request for holy communion, he had called ahead of time for one of the chaplains or pastoral assistant to bring his holy communion. When I got to his room, he was extremely happy to see me, he knew I brought what he requested, but in other to create a friendship bond, I asked the client whether he was happy to see me for me or he was happy to see me because I brought something valuable with me.

The client replied" Both" we both busted laughing, he was a good person. I then asked him, whether he was ready to receive the communion, he reply "Yes", table was prepared and we said the prayer and he received the communion, after the activity, he requested for a short prayer, using the "invitation method" of praying, I told him with his own mouth to ask God for his blessing and that I will join him with grace and Lord's prayer, he obliged. The prayer went well, and he was happy he did that for himself with a witness,

I emphasized that where two or three are gathered our Lord is always present, the patient agreed. We talked, he told me, he could no longer do things for himself anymore due to sickness, and that it was indeed hard to depend on other people for help. I assured him, that sometimes we just have to do that to allow others to serve us, nothing is wrong with that, all of us just have to recognize that and give God the honor for having put someone in our path to assist when we needed it the most, and he should not look at it that way, but thank God, help was available. He was grateful for all we did for him at the hospital, both his medical team people and our department. I remembered that day, my patient said, my name if I don't see you anymore because, they are going to discharge me this evening to the nursing home. Thank you so much for visiting me, we both hugged each other.

Hospital Visit Client Number Eight

The second client today was a 42 years old Hispanic male. He requested for "anointing of the sick" due to pending surgical procedure the following Monday. I informed him that I have requested for the pastor, the on-call pastor will have to perform it. The wife was happy. The patient was so happy with his treatment so far, he complimented the doctors, the nurses the techs and our department. I gave him our department number, informed him, he can called 24/7 and someone will pick up the phone, and he can request prayer any time of the day. He thanked me, and I left.

Hospital Visit-Client Number Nine

God is good, all the time. All the time God is good. To have met this person, you know God is the owner of the universe. And Jesus is the Rock we all stand. This individual revealed to me, that she never had too many friends, she was very outspoken, she might have offended them if she spoke her mind, at such never had a meaning relationship with people, at 63 year old. we talked, she told me the meaning of my name, she talked about her favorite saints and some spiritual leaders who she admired and still living to my amazement.

She even told me her candid encounter with the scented aroma of beautiful virgin Mary as she walked through the Garden in our Lady of Sacred Heart in Chicago. She visited fifteen Cathedrals while on vacation in Chicago, she said she did that for herself, ever since her illness was unpredictable now, her way of thanking God for her life.

We joked that Houston only have one Co-cathedral, she came from another State for treatment. She said, some people saw what she saw but afraid, they might think they're coo, so the information never gets out or shared. I told the patient that whatever she saw, if that enable her to seek God more, then she should not allow others to take it away from her, because that become her experience, I can't disapprove her own vision, just as she can't disapprove my own vision.

All I know is God is good, and He revealed Himself to whom He wanted to reveal Himself to. and I reminded her about Martha and Mary. Marth was cooking and washing pans and dishes, her sister

Mary sat at our Lord's feet gaining insights into Heavenly Kingdom and when Martha complaint to Jesus our Lord said "

As Jesus and his disciples were on their way, he came to a village where a woman named Martha opened her home to him. She had a sister called Mary, who sat at the Lord's feet listening to what he said. But Martha was distracted by all the preparations that had to be made. She came to him and asked, "Lord, don't you care that my sister has left me to do the work by myself? Tell her to help me!"

"Martha, Martha," the Lord answered, "you are worried and upset about many things, but few things are needed-or indeed only one. Mary has chosen what is better, and it will not be taken away from her." (Luke 10:38-42). So, I told the patient, I have to pass on that, I will not have a comment, but what she told me, I believed her. I told her what I saw many years ago but kept quiet. A lot of Christians are afraid to share information of their encounters, nobody will believe them. Miracles happened every day, we thanked one another. Oh, taste and see the goodness of our Lord, oh taste and see, the goodness of our Lord, our Lord. we sang and departed from each other. What a visit.

Hospital Visit Client Number Ten 01/15/2016

I met this young man today, age 22 years old, very articulate, we both introduced ourselves. He did not ask for anything. I asked him, he was too young to be here, he laughed, he said Agnes I got sick, came to ER, but the hospital kept me for a precaution purpose, I hope to go home within two or three days, if they did not find anything. The young man mother at bedside for support. Both of them thanked me for coming and thanked my department.

Hospital Visit-Client Number Eleven

I met a young lady today, 43 years old, very pleasant, her room window /curtain was pulled, it was total darkness in that room. I asked if she 's ok. She said, she was fine, but I knew something was wrong, something indeed was wrong, her husband was at bedside, and since her significant other was there I chose not to probe her for answer. I asked both of them if we can pray together, both said yes. We held hands and prayed. she had requested for communion, she wanted it and I gave it. I thanked both of them, and we parted.

Hospital Visit-Client Number Twelve 02/14/2016

I met this 85 years old man today, he smiled as I introduced myself, and the daughter was also at bedside visiting. I asked if he needed, or want anything from my department, yesterday he requested for a Bible and I brought it today, he wanted to take it with him to the nursing home on Monday. He also requested for "Anointing of the sick" for Monday before going back to nursing home and holy water from the pastor, I told him that the pastor will bring those on Monday since the department had put his name down. He was happy that his needs will be met. We said the Lord's prayer and the grace together and I left the room.

Hospital Visit-Client Number Thirteen 02/14/2016.

I went to fourteen floor today to see a seventy-seven years old female. She was very pleasant, she requested for a priest confession, she was adamant and forceful to see the priest. I told her only a priest or pastor ordained can perform this request. She requested for information on the penitent act prayer cards, provided with some other religious materials, told her the priest will come as soon as one is available. I thanked her and left for the day.

Hospital Visit Client Number Fourteen 02/14/2016

I met this 75 years old man who came to the hospital from East Texas to Houston, 100 miles away from home to medical center. He requested a Bible, prayer cards, and communion. I got to his room, introduced myself, he introduced himself and a bond was developed. He was an elderly person with very good sense of humor.

Wife and children at bedside visiting. He told me one of his regret in life was he was not forceful or push his children into Catholicism, but they're old now in another faith, baptism. I could not understand why they have to think it was their faults, especially if you have an adult child, they can make up their minds, at least both of your Children are Christians, you should be proud that at least they belong to Jesus, on the judgement day-Our Lord will not ask your church membership, but how well you serve him and your brothers and sisters. We must be careful not to dwell too much on where we worship and then end up losing Eternity.

Our soul is more valuable than that. One of the children at bedside told the parents that they should not feel that they have failed the children while growing up. In Jesus there is forgiveness and trust. Nobody should make another person feel ashamed where they worship, we should encourage each other.

I served the holy communion, we prayed, and we thanked the Lord, and I also thanked the family for allowing me into their family dynamic/struggles. Parents should pray for their adult children and asked God that whatever the children do, the Lord will bless them, and they should make rightful decision.

Hospital Visit Client Number Fifteen 09/18/2015.

Today I met a 85 years old woman good nature she greeted with humility and she was very happy to be alive at that age. She told me every day is a blessing, I brought her communion because she had requested it ahead of time. she told me as a young person, she was a poet, and she had appeared and wrote many plays for theater. she now lived in a nursing home in Texas, and in couple of days she will go back. she asked me about my family, I told her.

She pulled a plastic bag out sitting on the chair in her room, told me to take three papers out and go to the nursing station and copy it for her. She told me at the conclusion of the meeting that she had no regrets, she lived a well lived life, and thank God every day.

she said she wrote all her poems for Jesus and she was waiting for someone from our department to show up, and I walked in, we both laughed, and a bond developed instantaneously.

A Jewish girl from New York, We both laughed. Meeting this patient today, was a God sent, she shared her inner thoughts with me as a Jewish girl growing up in New York, her only escape was her work and writings., we shared our inner thought naturally, and after wards it felt wonderfully. Inspite of our age different, we were able to interact   peacefully at bedside without hesitation. A heavenly inheritance we both shared.

Hospital Visit Client Number Sixteen 01/13/2017

My visit today was regular visit. I visited twenty-two patients, but three stood out for me, a nineteen year, a sixty-seven and sixty-eight years old. Each visit and patient encounter have always been as unique as God Almighty made each and every one of us to be. We are very special and our uniqueness always point to God our creator, these three people today were special, not all visit will be cut and dry, some visit and the nature of visit will be as unique as ever, some visit will be fifteen to 20minutes at the most, and some special occasion it could be an hour depending on what the patient has to share with follow-ups from department of Chaplaincy and spiritual care services.

The first patient I saw today was a nineteen-year-old, he had requested for communion to be brought to him in his room. I had prepared the communion and ready to serve, As I got to the room, and I asked him whether he's ready to receive the communion, he told me, he meant on Sunday. I told him I would have to change his card to Sunday only. When the young man called the spiritual care department, he did not specify which day of the week, so computer had him down daily, so I told him my department has to go back and change the order.

This young man was surprise that the hospital in now automated, and not only could they look at the time he received one, they could go back and check the Sacrament book and validated who provided him one. I told the young man that the spiritual care department is part of his care too while in the hospital and he can assess the department 24/seven, someone will be able to respond to his need and that on-call people are in the hospital for an emergency for the families. As we talked, he changed his mind, that since I have the communion with me, he might as well take it, since he did not know for sure, which floor he will end up in the morning, as we were talking, the young man mother came in, and she too received a communion, they were both happy.

The mother told me to not change anything from his card, and that it appeared they were going to be here for another week. The young man requested for a prayer and a Bible, which I provided. The visit was a very pleasant one, I thanked both of them and left our card to them.

Hospital Visit Client Number Seventeen 1 /13/ 2017

The second patient today was a sixty-seven years old man, as I walk to his room, his daughter was getting him ready for a walk in the hallway. His daughter told me to come back, but he disagreed that, He had been waiting for me almost ten minutes that he did not tell his daughter that I might missed him when I come, and he said my timing was just perfect and he's ready for his communion and the holy water in an 4oz bottle prepared and blessed by our pastor in our department. This time, the daughter stepped out of the room and waited in visitor lounge, as I was getting the communion out, I slipped, almost fell but the communion did not break either, he was so happy that He acclaimed "God is good". And out of spontaneity I said back to him "All the time" we both were having great time. Very nice and knowledgeable man, he also requested for prayer and we prayed with the healing psalm 3:3-5, and we concluded with the Lord's prayer. He thanked me for coming, and I in turn gave him our department card. Then I went back to visitor lounge to tell the daughter she could go in now, the daughter thanked me and our department for the work we do.

Hospital Visit Client Number Eighteen 1/13/2017

The moment t I entered this patient room, I knew he had been waiting for our department to show –up. Before I even step into his room, he was asking whether I have time to speak with him, and my answer was yes.

He said the reason he asked that was he's going need more than the usual time, we both laughed. One of the reasons we visit the sick, is to allow them to voice their inner concern which they could not share with either the doctors or nurses, some of them feel that, they're imposing or the questions could be view as embarrassing to them or the nurses might think they're silly but for any spiritual questions nothing is silly or negative, we go with the patients together with the word of God, and retrieve the information for them, we are just their guide, a friend in need, a brother or sister.

Our job at bedside is not to pass judgement on anybody, we assist them to cope and provide answers for them during spiritual distress, We listen to their inner concerns and the doctors read our note for those doctors who consulted spiritual care department to manage their patient's spirituality for them, for better patient outcome. Today my client told me to sit and he has something to tell me. Here is the dialogue: The main purpose of this patient's interaction with a hospital minister is to show that in any given visit, nobody can predict how the patients would receive us each day, some of the patients, the visit at bedside will be between ten to twenty minutes, and to some a lengthy one perhaps an hour, but all and all we always thanked them for allowing us to come into their boats and journeyed with them.

7.9c Verbatim: Patient and Pastoral Minister

Patient: I was sad and depressed today, after the doctor told me I will have to stay for another eight weeks in the hospital. I asked him why? The "Heart Team" told me I will need to replace my heart with artificial one and wait until a new heart could be found, that will take another week, my name is already on the transplant list.

Pastoral Minister: So, you're depressed because of the wait, or you're depressed because you're having a guilty conscience?

Patient: - I am depressed because as a Christian, I do not want anybody to die so that I can have the individual heart.

Pastoral Minister: - Are you scare or fearful that the procedure will not be successful, and you can still die anyway.

Patient: - Yes, the fear of unworthiness, the helplessness, that for the first time in my life, I felt hopeless and helpless. I could not control my life and destiny that it has come to this.

Pastoral Minister: - That It has come to asking or somebody has to die for you to live?

Pastoral Minister: - Is it because, all your life, you have always make decision for others whether it is in your family or at your work

Patient: - Yes, I have always in control of all aspect of my life.

Pastoral Minister: - But now, others Are making it for you-for examples, your doctors, your nurses, dieticians, and others, but not you?

Patient: - Yes

Pastoral Minister: - Do you know part of our journey too is, if we live long enough, others will have to help us, there is nothing wrong with that, do you know also that, there is also a season for that in the sacred text for example in Ecclesiastes 3:1-5.

Do you also know that Moses took the advice of his father in-law to have others to assist him, because he was overwhelmed with task, and he listened and called the elders together and put those who are capable, trust worthy in a position of judges? And God Almighty told him Bravo for sharing his gift with others.

To allow others to help during crisis has not diminish us, it empowered us that God put somebody in a position to help us, our capacity to Love and ask Jesus to help us at this time in our life should be the focus and our prayer for God help and we ought to pray for those medical people for God to help them on your behalf, and pray for the family who will donate that organ for you that the good Lord will bless them also and what they lost, they will regain and move on to do better things in life, instead of worrying yourself. Is okay to worry and contemplate, but it should not take a whole of time, and space.

Jesus told us, by worrying can anyone add a day to his allotted time on earth.? What you need to is prayer ask God to take this complicated issues and sickness from your hand and turn it to triumph and be witness for Jesus. Hand over the care to Jesus, believe and have faith. Do not worry so much for those who provided the donation, pray for them, even though you do not know them. Do not limit our God's healing graces upon you. Let Jesus be Jesus, Believe Him.

Do not hinder or oppose your own blessing. Do you know if you refuse the donation, the organ goes to another person? Just relax and pray for the "Heart Team" and for suitable donor.

Patient: - Whoa, I never thought about all these scenario I'm glad you came by. Can I get a Bible?

Pastoral Minister: Yes, but let me go back to my department. I will check for you.

Patient: - Thank you

CHAPTER 8:
Can Adults Define Their Purpose in Life.

Of course, if we look at the world purposely, another task confronting seniors is the challenge of locating new sources of fulfillment and joy when jobs, careers and family no longer dictate how our time is spent and give shape to our identity. What gives us meaning and satisfaction? From whence do we derive our purpose for living? What are we if we are not industrious? If we are no longer "producers" of income or healthy children and families, what is our role?

Our early and middle adult years do not adequately prepare us for the new role of being an older adult. Shifting out of the role we are groomed for and into the unfamiliar role of retiree and then well elderly person may produce feelings of despair and depression.

Dependency is difficult no matter what our age. But loss of independence isn't the only form of loss that we may experience. As our abilities change, there may also be a growing feeling of helplessness from oneself, a disconnect, if you will, between our self-perception and our physical reality. Maslow Hierarchy of needs kind of summarized the nightmare a lot of elderly folk's face, some were forced to look at their life's worth and doubt their abilities and self-worth in materialistic way, but not in spirituality sense of real perception. Some animated their worth with false sense of who they're really are, when you talk to them at bedside, you begin to wonder as a neutral eye, if only these people can actually see how much they're worth as children of God aside the worldly acquisition, if only they knew, but our society have placed a huge bounty on our heads which God Almighty did not put there, human being have been reduced to total automation, performance appraisal, anything less than you're a loser. Christians have to be careful too in the midst of this "Showboat".

Most of these sickness or death could have been prevented only if people add two and two together. Our Lord told us to let His grace be sufficient for us, it means whatever your status in life, we should be happy, our nation is the most blessed nation on earth, yet we die very soon due to overwork, and not being smart as our Lord told us to. We have to find that which enriches us, there a lot of people my generation, 50-60 years old who have their vocation already given to them but still looking for them. We have to pray so that Jesus can reveal them to us.

Most of us are not trained with the understanding that we are each temporarily able; that life's accidents and injuries and the process aging will alter our physical and cognitive functioning. And so, as our abilities are impaired, our body ceases to be a place of familiarity, comfort and ease. If our physical and cognitive functioning is no longer predictable and reliable, we no longer know our body. And who are we then? P lease indulge me to gentle walk you through these real-life events with a nurse and her dying patients. The nurse has carefully selected these seven patients for this project.

8.1 Mission And Ministry No One Dies Alone Tonight
A Nurse and Her Clients

Are there other ways one can come to terms with the end of one's life without having a religious belief?

I imagine so, but I believe that no matter what we call it, we are having a religious or spiritual experience all of the time. So, what one person may call a strictly secular experience I may see as the day-to-day presence of the holy or the mystery of life. (Brower 2006).

No matter what we call it, if an event or experience moves us to a feeling of awe or opens us to seeing a glimmer of goodness that encourages our faith, as described previously, we are attuned to a quality of being and living that will help us cope with whatever may come.

Everybody need a place to start, we need each other, which means we have to start somewhere from our community, we need the church or religion affiliates to get us going, none of us can come to Jesus without other members, remember the second commandments in which Jesus said, love your neighbor as yourself, our neighbor is each other, we can't exclude others, but include(Them) others at the end of the journey. We have to be truthful to the faith.

The New Testament says that every believer is a ministering priest who is to be ministering to the common good of the body of Christ according to the gifts and talents God has given us. I used to think about myself having no gifts, and I really don't know what I'm doing, until one day I went to church and start inquiring what I can do as A lay person, I volunteered as Window washer at my church, after about six-week Jesus upgraded me to go to school for hospital pastoral minister. Jesus said you're a nurse, And I have already positioned you in the hospital role, I let the Spirit of the Lord directed my path. For years I ran away or almost gave up my calling thinking my job will secure my place in Heaven, Here I was again with entitlement, telling God, Iam a good person, have a job, family that love God, paid taxes, never once in trouble with the law, so Lord I'm a good person.

But never once ask God what is it that He wanted me to do for Him? When I arrived at the interview session for the hospital ministry to start my training, the pastor that interviewed me was not a pastor from my church. The program I'm going for is an" interfaith mission" at the time, I have no clue the pastor interviewing me wanted to know whether I was ready for my discernment or not, that time I really don't know the scholarly definition of the word, I just knew God wanted me there, and I hope I got in.

After the interview, He ask me whether I have any questions and I replied yes. My question to the pastor/Reverend that day was," how come all these years I never pick up a flyer in the CCE section after church service ?

Well for the first time in your adult life replied the pastor, you allowed Jesus into your boat, and He opened the veil for you, so now you can see. I did the interview, never thought about it, and went about my life, and four weeks later I was admitted into the program. What I'm trying to say is sometimes we need the church to help us to fulfil our God's given talents, and other times we can be a channel of grace to people but Jesus work with that individuals for that purpose.

After volunteering our time with others, we need somewhere to also go for spiritual advisement/counseling, as Jesus said, don't rely on your own counsel in (NIV, Proverbs. 3.1-6). Most of the people I visited on a weekly basis were my brothers and my sisters in Christ, the patients in the hospital came from our communities and around the world, even though we speak different dialect and languages, we speak the same language of God.

They have allowed me to come to their boat, and I also allowed them to come inside my boat through mutual respect and sharing of God's message at bedside. God is good to us with our "Gifts of Time". Gifts constitutes God's primary place of ministry for believers. Gifts are declaration of God's will and calling for our lives. (NIV, Romans. 12.2-3).

All believers are to show mercy, give, walk by faith, and help others, most believers have special gifts which enable them to excel in each of these areas, (NASB, Romans. 12.7-8). And 1 Corinthians. 12. 9, 28). Again, where and how we are to use our gifts is a matter of God's individual leading and whether or not we are listening to His leading. (NASB, Corinthians. 12.4-6)." Now there are varieties of gifts, but the same Spirit. 5And there are varieties of ministries, and the same Lord. 6 There are varieties of effects, but the same God who works all things in all person".

Question: You have your own personal story concerning how a healing, a peace, can come near the end of life.

Yes, through my mother's living with debilitating illness and her process of dying I learned that, generally speaking, people die the way they live, with the same attitudes and biases and defenses in place, but that the possibility of personal growth, revelation, healing and "transformation exists right up until the very last breath is drawn" (Brower 2006).

My mother lived with my youngest sister, the day she fell I received a call from her, but she never told me it was a bad fall, she thought she could handle it, but a week later she passed away. I was not there to say the last goodbye to my mother, I knew she lived a good decent life and at the time of death, she was surrounded by her family, and I did talk to my mother on the phone a day before her passing, I told one of the family to put the phone to her ears, one family told me she could not hear but in a coma, but I insisted and the phone was placed into her ear and I told her I loved her and I thanked her for everything she ever did for me, and I personally released her of her earthly duties as my mother that If God called her, she should embraced Him and go with Him. Our hearing is the last to go even when in a coma, as a nurse I knew that. Iam glad I sung her favorite song to her that day, those who were at bedside said my mother face lights up during the singing and another family asked who was on the phone and someone said it was I. The family expressed the information during her eulogy.

8.2 Client Number One No One Dies Alone Tonight 01/19/2017

I got to work today, I never expected anything but do my job to the best of my ability. I had three patients tonight. One of my patient came from IMU to ICU tonight for 24Hours observation due to her diagnosis and prognosis, a cardiac pt. with pacemaker. I went to each patient, introduced myself, sometimes the families are with them being in ICU, then exited the care area at night for home or to Lobby areas. When I got to ICU bed #6, she was all alone, her daughter had gone home for the night only to come back again in the morning. I introduced myself, and patient confirmed her name on the armband. She was a seventy-four years old, very beautiful woman, she never looked her age at all. I informed her that, the next time for her medication will be at 2100, and I will bring them at that time. She requested a glass of water with the med when iam bringing the medication, and I told her "OK". We talked, and a bond quickly developed between her and myself. she further explained all the tests they performed with her throughout the day, she requested from me an incontinence brief, I told my patient that I will have to call the supervisor for that since we do not carry those per ICU-level supplies cart, patient said, Alright. I got the brief from the supervisor, patient helped me to put it on I assisted a little, we talked some more, throughout the night, I will go to her room to share her up. At around 2300, I went again to check upon her.

This is where I asked again, if she's "OK" just doing my job and I do not mean to be intrusive as a nurse, patient grab my hand and said; "Agnes, pray for me with a smile, then I asked; what's going on? She wore on her right arm a brace, the history said, she fell at home and broke the arm in August of last year (8/22/2016), she corrected me, it actually happened in June 2016, and had never healed, but now I have a tremendous pain each time I moved to do my daily activities. patient also had a history of dementia, and she uses oxygen @ 2L/NC continuously. I told the patient, I will put her in my prayer. The night went fine, no incident.

At about 0600, I went to inform her that today, she will go back to IMU, since all her test came back, she's doing fine, and the heart doctor said she can go back to her unit, patient was very happy. At 0730, before leaving for home, I went and brought her fresh iced water since she loved drinking water and told her bye for the day.

I came back the following night, which was on 1/20/17. I got to my unit, but patient had already left for IMU as the transferred paper had been signed by the doctor earlier that day. I never thought anything off it.

Tonight, my extra duty aside my assigned duty will be to be part of Code-Team tonight as an ICU- nurse, meaning if there is any code page tonight I must respond and attend the code.

As I finished my 2100 med passed to patient, a code-page came overhead, Code blue room 303, code-blue IMU-303. I grabbed the portable Code –blue supplies bag, then went downstairs to the room. I attached the electrode/pacing wires, we could not shock because patient had a pacemaker already, we gave cardiac medication and performed CPR, and patient was my patient last night in ICU. We tried to resuscitated her but no luck, her daughter told us to stop the CPR and let her go, and we stopped the chest compression/cardiac drips. MD time of death 2132.

Client Number Two No One Dies Alone Tonight 11/27/2011

I received my assignment tonight. My patient was a 70 years old female.   According to shift report, pt. coded three days ago, she remains on vasopressors-meaning receiving heart medications which was keeping her alive. Family have not decided whether to place her on "DNR" status, but for now, we do everything medically available for her. My patient status remained guarded. Patient daughter at bedside, she was at bedside all day, MD again told her the prognosis and the fact that, if she coded again, the team may or may not be able to bring her back, due to severity of the illness. Patient daughter asked the doctor to sign with her the "DNR" paperwork.

. Patient daughter told the nursing personnel's and MD as long as we do the best we could, we should let her go, if we have tried our best. After the daughter finished signing the DNR papers, she requested I joined her at her mother's room for a prayer. I obliged. She led the prayer, and I assisted also. I knew from her eye, she was happy to do that for her mother. An hour later a code-was called but a silence one, because the family changed their mind to "DNR" but allowed a silence passage, with dignity of a human person". This night, her daughter was at bedside, did not question the event, but allowed God to intervene and grab her mother hands, the scene was serene, quiet, all probes, monitoring equipment removed, room was so quiet, peaceful.

One nurse that had been taking care of the patient and knew the deceased patient said, whoa, "we finally allowed her to go", and she said, that woman had been dead three days ago, but the science kept her alive for three days until her daughter came terms with the illness and with God. She said later Amazing; we all turn back to the nurse and said "Whoa".

Daughter provided me with the funeral home number, the grieving process began with family and their loved ones, and I called the funeral home, and couples of nurses help me with post-mortem care. Patient daughter called other relatives, to come to hospital to say their own good byes, she was ready for the family, every one of them said their byes and the body left our hospital before midnight. It was one of the best care I ever witnessed and participated, after is said and done, family came forward and took ownership of after death care. Even though the event was a sad one, but it was celebrated joyfully, Mrs. M, daughter celebrated her mother life and the hospital staff assisted her, and God is glorified. (Proverbs 16:1-4). "The plans of the heart belong to man, but the answer of the tongue is from the Lord. All the ways of a man are pure in his own eyes, but the Lord weighs the Spirit, commit your work to the Lord, and your plans will be established. The Lord has made everything for its purpose, even the wicked for the day of trouble".

Client Number Three No One Dies Alone Tonight 02/14/2016

Today is Valentine's Day. Across America and around the world people celebrated the day of LOVE which is the first name of our

LORD. God love the world so much that He gave His beloved Son –Jesus to us, for repentance of our sins. We celebrated with "RED ROSES" today for those who have love in their heart. A fictional character Romeo and Juliet a lover, novel written by a person, brought to us by us, and whole world celebrated this day for the beauty being in love. What a phenomenon. The whole world is in love today.

I got to work tonight, my shift starts from 7pm to 7am. I picked my assignment tonight, but one patient was added instead of one taking off, because I had three patients the previous night, usually whoever had three patients for two days, on their third nights the supervisor dropped one patient to allow the nurse lower loads for third night, mine was not the case tonight. Another patient was added, I saw it, but decided I will just let it go and do my best.

The patient I was assigned tonight was on ventilator, a seventy-two years old man. Patient has history of respiratory failure, he was on a ventilator, his condition and medical status remained guarded, after the shift report, I went straight to the room. I introduced myself to the family, told them I am the nurse assigned to their loved one, if they needed anything throughout the night while they stayed with the patient, they should let me know, patient wife said OK". At 2100, all night-time meds passed without incident, went to monitoring tech to keep extra eye on my patient for me tonight, because of the report I got during shift change that patient condition throughout the day was serious and guarded, and he still remains "Full-Code" status.

There was no any noticeable changing in cardiac rhythm until around 0325, we had just cleaned the patient, because she had a loose bowel movement, four nurse were helping me with turning and changing, then we discovered this change on the monitor, so we quickly stopped what we were doing and called the house MD to come to bedside, patient already had all cardiac ivs maximal-out, meaning the intravenous fluids rates of all meds have been reached, patient was on continuous drips. My patient weigh 397.7 pounds on specialty bed. His heart rate was significantly low, so we called" code-blue". Before the wife left that night around mid-night, she told me (Nurse) that I can call her anytime. We started the code at around 0325 and we stopped at about 0337.

Patient wife told the Medical doctor during code to stop the code, that "Enough is Enough" let him go". All this time as we continued the CPR wife was on the way to the hospital with her daughter driving. As soon as the wife came into the room, she told the medical doctor present at the code scene to stop, and we did just that. We stopped the CPR and discontinued all meds, less than one minute, patient had flat line on the monitor, and MD called the time of death 0337. No response, pulpit fixed and dilated, no b/p, no respiration, everything was silent now. Mrs. P came in, went straight to her husband and kissed him on the cheek, the staff lost it, and staff started crying. Tonight, was the first time I ever worked with them, from the moment I saw the family, and I knew that they were good people, friendly and approachable.

The wife gave us go ahead to clean him up for other family to come in and said their good byes, three nurses stayed with me and helped me with post-mortem care. Mr. P departed to the Lord on 2/15/2016 at 0337. One of the joy I witnessed at his bedside today was, the wife never left his side, with the occasion of going home to sleep and come back the following morning with our facility for six weeks, and patient had been in so many hospitals before coming to us.

She stopped the code because, she saw in his eyes the pain and the struggle each day, and he no longer recognized them. Patient wife told me that during the day on 2/14/2016, the valentine Sunday, all but one grandchildren could not visit him due to age, A family picture was taken at bedside that afternoon. The wife told me, because I asked, if the husband was a Christian, and she said yes a Baptist, so we called other nurses to come back to the room to pray with family before the funeral home took the body away.

The wife was so happy we did that for them. We prayed for the faithful departed, and the family, and we closed with the Lord's prayer. Within one hour the body was released to the funeral home and the family left the hospital.

Client Number Four No One Dies Alone Tonight
A Family Decision 11/16/2015

Tonight, my assignment was a seventy-two-year-old male, in ICU-bed number 14. My report indicated, he was very sick and on multiples iv drips. I immediately went to his room, to check him out and performed my own shift assessment, made sure everything I needed was well stocked in the room, patient was a "Full Code" status and no family members at bedside.

According to the report I got from the morning nurse, many attempts were made during that shift to the family regarding the End-of-life – crisis to obtain "DNR" status because patient coded twice during the day, but the family told the medical personnel to do everything for the patient, after successful resuscitation, patient was now on ventilator with multiples iv drips, and no family at bedside today. My first night with the patient ended, but the status remained serious and guarded-meaning patient was unstable, and anything can happen anytime, life and death loomed. I gave report to the morning nurse and informed her everything I did overnight and what needed to be continued and followed up. I left the unit at about 0800.

Client Number Four Second Night Room 14

I got to the hospital tonight, hoping that my assignment would change, and picked up another patient, but instead, due to continuation of care, I got my patient back, patient remained intubated and still on ventilation. He coded again during the day at around 11:25AM, and another time at 12:05pm. Patient's non-responsive to name or environment any more. Wife was notified on the phone with update according to shift report, the day time nurse found out that wife went to Vegas for Family event, and patient son could come to the hospital if needed, the day time nurse obtained consent for "No CPR" only chemical code now, no chest compression any more. wife told the day time nurse that, she had to change her ticket to emergency at the ticket counter and she will be in Houston the next day. Patient asked the day time nurse to keep the patient alive until she got home and decide how to proceed with care. In the meantime, our focus was to help and care for the patient.

My shift ended, and we continued to help the patient, doctors and technicians were all aware of treatment and plan of care for the patient.

Client Number Four Third Night No One Dies Alone Tonight
A Family Decision

My patient condition worsened, wife arrived from the airport and came straight to the hospital with her son and one family member. Wife saw the husband, talked with her son and the other family at bedside, told me to excuse them while they (family) deliberated, about fifteen minutes wife called me back to the room asked about all the other options available to make a life and death decision on behalf of her husband.

At that time, I told her that I needed the supervisor to hear the conversation and provided her all options available. I then called the supervisor and the house MD to bedside to hear what the family got to say. Pt family had elected to terminate life and choose the hospice route. The supervisor gave the patient wife all necessary papers to fill out while the house MD was at bedside with patient. patient wife signed the paper, house MD signed his own side of document. I witnessed the signing of the signature as a primary nurse taking care of this patient.

At 2200, house MD called the primary care physician and informed him what the family wanted, primary care physician said ok, and the stage was set to take patient off life-support, all life-supporting equipment will be turned off. At 2210, all medical personnel's gathered at patient bedside, with wife, son and sister, I informed the wife to say good bye now and if the family wished to say a pray this is the moment now before the MD turn them off, she did , and I excused myself from the room.

At 2216, patients was extubated, meaning removing from life's support monitors and tubes and breathing machine. And less than 20 minutes patient died. Time of death 2240 by House MD. Primary care physician called by house Doctor for time of death. Family at bedside. One family member remarked and said, at last no more suffering and pain. Wife gave me a funeral home to call.   At 2255, funeral home called that they're on their way. And by 2333, body was released to the funeral home for burial.

The decision to "Let Go" a family member in any End-of-life-crisis should not be taken lightly, I saw how today, how people struggled with this decision, and it is never a joke, or a simple matter, I saw today in that room that family considered all option available by law to them, and I also saw how medical personnel's wrestled with this decision, the sadness involved but necessary option for the family and the patient. What really bore down to was the "Quality of Life "of that individual person.

The decision was solely on the family, and we have to respect their values, beliefs and responsibilities to one another. We owe no judgement to no one, we asked God to help each and every one of us in this life journey, because life and death is in the hand of our Lord. We can only hope that the deceased lived a blessed life, and may we all meet Jesus on the resurrection day in His Kingdom, Amen.

Client Number Five No One Dies Alone Tonight
A Family Decision 09/24/2014.

I received a call that one of our pastors wanted me to go to a funeral ceremony with him as a pastoral assistant as soon as I finished my visiting with the patients on my floors. One of the patients at St. Luke's hospital had died, and we have visited the individual while alive. The daughter of the deceased contacted our department if a pastor would be available to follow them to the graveyard for necessary ceremony. AS a pastoral assistant, I told the Reverend I will meet him at the graveyard, he texted me the name and location.

I got there at about 1pm. The family and the Reverend were already waiting for me to arrive, What the daughter wanted was to have a Reverend bless her mother Ashes and place it in the space allotted them.

The service was nice and short, only 30 minutes, in attendance were-the daughter, the grandson, Reverend and myself and the deceased. We sang, I read the Bible passage, and Reverend talked about the reason why we came.

This event was the best I ever witnessed, not only was it short, but the sweetest in the sense that-it was purely family affairs, the daughter told me, this was how her mother wanted it, and before she passed away, she got permission for cremation from her church. And I thought to myself, Amazing.

Going to this funeral that day, I never thought much about it, until the deceased daughter told me what her mother wanted and needed, I was so impressed that even after the deceased had passed away, she was still part of her care, by making her will known to her family, and I thanked them for inviting me. Indeed, it was a blessed day. we take thing or each other for granted, but when the ship comes to shore, may we be wise and have God wisdom and understanding. Amen. Let us listen to Apostle Paul message here.

1. God will give us strength.

But his answer was: "My grace is all you need, for my power is greatest when you are weak." I am most happy, then, to be proud of my weaknesses, in order to feel the protection of Christ's power over me. – (NIV, 2 Corinthians. 12.9).

Client Number Six No One Dies Alone Tonight
A Family Decision 07/02/2017.

I received my assignment tonight without making any thing out of it, never anticipated that my patient in ICU bed one, will be the toughest assignment yet. This patient was 62 year old, came from IMU via in-house transfer due to low blood pressure and diarrhea. patient was talking, there were no visible signs of problem at beginning of the shift. Family was at bedside during the shift change and report.

Since I have no prior knowledge of the patient and family. I went straight to the room to introduce myself to patient and family. A beautiful bond developed quickly, very nice family, I told them to call me immediately if they needed help, the oldest daughter told me ok. My patients had four girls, and they have followed and assisted their mother with taking care of their dad while in the hospital. Each night, one daughter will have stayed behind to support their dad, while the rest went with their mother each night.

The arrangement was very nice. Tonight being my first time with them, the oldest daughter gave me the phone numbers of other siblings, I quickly went and secure the number in patient's chart. At around midnight, the family left for home, but before e they left, the oldest child told me, if he ever coded or needed emergency care, I should call her immediately. I told her ok, so they left.

At around 0130, during my round, I noticed patient respiration became labored, even though patient was on life support and machine breathing for him, so I called the respiratory therapist to the room immediately, she came and saw what I saw, before we could even blink our eyes, I pulled the code button.

Code was called while in the room and then the code team arrived, called the family to come quickly due to change in patient status. Less than 30minutes, the relatives were at bedside, as the code was in progress, the family prayed outside the patient room and promised never to disturbed us or be in our way, patient's code status was "Full Code" … for this particular patient, it was the longest run code recorded in our ICU history, more than 20 minutes, even though family were present, they could not bring themselves to let go, and the code never ended.

The patient children that day acted as an intercessory prayer warrior on behalf of their father asking God to spare their dad for unfinished business. The following day, the children told everyone that they loved their father so much, and that he was a good father, and while growing-up he was their role model.

Three days later my patient was doing so well, and nobody could believe he had coded back to back three days before. The family made a decision that day that, next time he coded, the nursing staff and medical staff should allow him to go, the new code status sheet was signed with "NO CPR", family told me, he had suffered too much, he had been sick for a long time, and they knew this time around, they might not be lucky to take him home.

A peaceful resolution was reached with their mother in the decision. We tried so much to help the deceased but the disease had advanced and nothing we can do again. Patient stayed for extra fifteen days after that night just enough time for family to come together and accepted the inevitable. Patient passed away on 07/19/2017 at 1705. The daytime nurse informed me when I got to work that night, that it was a peaceful passage. The family released his soul to our Lord for keeps.

Client Number Seven No One Dies Alone Tonight

I got to work tonight at 1845 as usual, I was given three patients, two of them on ventilator, meaning the machine was breathing for them, their diagnosis and prognosis were very bad, one patient for me came from IMU due to Shortness of Breath, so we place the patient on Bipap twenty-four hours observation, then she will eventually go back to IMU after a day, if her condition remains stable. I was introduced to one of my patient in ICU-bed 10, the nurse informed that the family always comes after work to visit and I should make necessary accommodation for them, because our visiting time ends at 9pm.

I told the daytime nurse okay and I thanked her, I finished my report and quickly did my shift assessment of my patients. On the kardex for this patient, she had been with us for four weeks, my first night taking care of her. The family came around 10pm, I allowed them to go in and visit, there was a young lady with the group, she asked if she could stay with her grandmother tonight, and that she will need me to wake her up around 0600 if she forgets to wake up, because she had to go to work. I said "Sure". I gave her blankets, water, juices and crackers.

At around 0200 during my round, the grand-daughter climbed her grand-mother bed slept with her with her arms on her shoulder, both slept snuggly, she did not disturb my monitoring devices and equipment. The scene was so beautiful and peaceful, I could not make myself to wake her up and tell her to step aside, even though I could do that because it was nurse's decision and judgement.

Both my patient and grand-daughter slept nicely, and the shift went fine, and the young lady thanked me and left for work the following morning. It was the last time, this young lady will see her grand-mother alive, she passed away while she was at work that day, and by the time she came back, her parent had already given the daytime nurse the name of the funeral home, and when I got to work that night, the report I received was, she coded around noon but never recovered from the code, and family stopped the code when they got to the scene and saw what the Healthcare workers and the MD did.

The importance of this scenario was I thanked God for allowing this young lady to stay with her overnight, nobody knows when our own time will come, but we pray that the good Lord will send us a companion on our last day on earth, I was glad that the Spirit of the Lord was with me that night to allow her to stay with her grand-mother. The family thanked me for allowing one of the grandchildren to stay with their mother, and I thanked them for allowing me to be part of their family struggles and crisis. No one dies alone tonight; our Lord is watching.

This is a journey that each and everyone us must take, we may have to suffer grief in all kinds of trials. These have come so that the proven genuineness of your faith … may result in praise, glory and honor when Jesus Christ is revealed. NIV, 1 Peter. 1.6-7, nobody is immune is part of life.

In the book of Mark, we read about a terrible storm. The disciples were with Jesus on a boat crossing the Sea of Galilee. When a "furious storm came up," the disciples—among them some seasoned fishermen were afraid for their lives (NIV, Mark.4.37-38). Did God not care? Weren't they handpicked by Jesus and closest to Him? Weren't they obeying Jesus who told them to "go over to the other side"? (v. 35). Why, then, were they going through such a turbulent time?

No one is exempt from the storms of life. But just as the disciples who initially feared the storm later came to revere Christ more, so the storms we face can bring us to a deeper knowledge of God. "Who is this," the disciples pondered, "even the wind and the waves obey him!" (v. 41). Through our trials we can learn that no storm is big enough to prevent God from accomplishing His will (NIV, Mark. 5.1).

While we may not understand why God allows trials to enter our lives, we thank Him that through them we can come to know who He is. We live to serve Him because He has preserved our lives. (Albert Lee).

Lord, I know I don't need to fear the storms of life around me. Help me to be calm because I stand secure in you. Amen.

8.3 The Storms of Life Prove The Strength of Our Anchor.

1. You are safe with God.

God is our refuge and strength. An ever-present help in trouble – (NIV, Psalm. 46.1)

2. God is in control.

He stilled the storm in a whisper, the wave of the sea was hushed – (NIV, Psalm. 107.29).

3. God will rescue you.

The righteous cry out, and the Lord hears them, he delivers them from all their troubles- (NIV, Psalm. 34.17).

4. Always trust in God as your protector.

He who dwells in the shelter of the Most High will rest in the shadow of the Almighty, I will say "of the Lord "He is my refuge and my fortress, my God in whom I trust." (NIV, Psalm. 91. 1-2).

5. God will give you strength

But He said to me," My grace is sufficient for you, for my power is made perfect in weakness, "Therefore, I will boast all the more gladly about my weakness, so that Christ's power may rest on me". (NIV, 2 Corinthians. 12.9).

We agreed that Our Lord is a good God, with humility, love and care, He shoulder our pain and suffering. Here is another Bible passage to make us feel invited with love, (NKJV, Matthew. 11.28-30).

28 Come to Me, all you who labor and are heavy laden, and I will give you rest. 29 Take My yoke upon you and learn from Me, for I am gentle and lowly in heart, and you will find rest for your souls. 30 For My yoke is easy and My burden is light."

We praise, and we honor his Holy name. We have to meet our

brothers and sisters where they're – Ministering is now where God's Children are, we have taken it to hospitals, we are moving and everywhere we are-Jesus is following His flocks. We thank all the pastors/reverends, brothers/sisters, chaplains, pastoral assistant and the lay leaders/persons who volunteer their talents and gifts for their ministry. Amen.

According to reverend (Brower, 2006). One of the essential elements that allowed any person to find that inner healing and peace, and to have a "good" death was the quality of care the individual received from the healthcare professionals, and from the hospital spiritual care team. No matter how old we get to be, no matter what the circumstances of our aging and dying, I believe that within our relationships with other people and through our unique experience of being alive, flashes of insight, moments of healing and transformation are always possible.

I encourage people to stay open to the fullness of experience, whether sorrowful or joyful, and the wisdom that will yet come to them, for through those deeply felt experiences, their life will be changed. And without love we are nothing (Billy Graham). (NIV, 1 Corinthians 13.1). Jesus said in. (NIV, John 13.35)." By this all we know that you are my disciples, if you have love for one another.

8.4 Heaven and Hell Are Real

This is not a hoax, nobody is exempt with this Divinely arrangement. God created Heaven and Hell, those who followed and obeyed Him while on Earth can have eternal bliss, and those who disobeyed His word while on Earth can equally have some where to go after life. He invited us to reserve our place time and time again while we can. These families' stories are not just their stories alone but our Lord's stories as well.

The End-of-life-crisis affected all people taking care of this individual persons at this particular moment in time. life is too short to delay following Jesus. Working as a bedside nurse for more than twenty years. I can tell you that in a twinkle of an eye, patient condition can change from good to extremely serious. Remember the famous Bible passage in (James 4:14 NIV). "A mist that appears for a little time and then vanishes".

So, every moment in life is precious". Again another Bible passage to give us an inspirational and perspective to what we have to deal with is found in (NIV, Ecclesiastes 3.1-4). A time for everything.

1 There is an appointed time for everything. And there is a time for every [a]event under heaven—

2 A time to give birth and a time to die;
  A time to plant and a time to uproot what is planted.

3 A time to kill and a time to heal;
  A time to tear down and a time to build up.

4 A time to weep and a time to laugh;
  A time to mourn and a time to dance.

8.5 Bereavement

Among the tasks set before the aging and the well elderly is the task of bereavement, the loss of some of their closest relationships.

If we live long enough, we may very well outlive our life companion. Not only must we cope with the emotional turmoil of deep grief and adjust to navigating the world alone, without someone who may have been by our side for most of our adult life, but the loss of our partner may send ripples out in all directions. For instance, without the support of our spouse, we may no longer be able to live

independently. We may need help with activities of daily living. We may need assistance with transportation. Or we may even be forced into a new and unfamiliar living arrangement, as in assisted living homes or nursing homes.

In addition to the sorrow and stress of mourning the death of a spouse, there is also the good possibility that as we age, we will experience a protracted period of grief as our circle of friends and family members die. Our social and familial support system may shrink to such an extent that we no longer feel "known." And one of our deepest human needs is the need for intimacy -- to be known and understood.

With the death of an older generation, and then our own age cohorts, we are left without people who knew us in all phases of our life and who experienced the same critical, life-shaping world events that shaped our life. As we find ourselves in the company of significantly younger people who do not share our frame of reference, we may feel increasingly alone and lonely. Which is why we must volunteer to serve others in our later years for fulfilment of God's hope, joy, grace and peace in us?

8.6 Grace and Commandment

Sanctifying Grace: This is a free gift of God which allows us to become children of God, to share in the divine nature, and to inherit eternal life. Through it, we put on Christ and live Christ life. The gift of sanctifying grace might be compare on a human level to the gift of human life.

1. Since we have human life, we can eat, hear, sense, smell, etc.

2. Just as with human life, there are certain powers or capabilities that comes with sanctifying grace, these are called virtues.

A virtue is a habit of doing what is good, just as a skilled pilot easily handles ordinary situations in the cockpit, so a virtuous person easily does what is good;

Sanctifying grace gives us the theological virtues of faith, hope and charity.

The theological virtues give us the grace to have a supernatural relationship with the Holy Trinity.

The theological virtue of faith, a gift given by God, enables us to believe in God and believe all that He has said and revealed to us, including all that church teaches. Faith is first and fore most an entrustment to God, a surrender of self to God.

The theological virtue of hope is a gift given by God, it enables us to desire eternal happiness and to trust in Christ and His promises the theological virtue of charity, a gift given by God it enables us to love God above all things for its own sake and our neighbor as ourselves for the love of God. In addition to the theological, sanctifying grace strengths and help us further develop the human virtues, also called moral virtues. The moral virtues are grouped around four key virtues called the cardinal virtues: prudence, justice, fortitude and temperance'

Prudence is the moral virtue by which we know our true good and choose the right means of achieving it Prudence perfects the intellect.

Justice is the moral virtue by which we give what is owed to God and others. The first and second commandment brings this to happen. Justice perfects the will.

Fortitude is the moral virtue by which we resist temptations and overcome obstacles. Fortitude helps us to moderate fear-courage factor.

Temperance is the moral virtue by which we moderate our desire for pleasurable goods; Temperance helps us to control our enjoyment of sensual pleasures. e.g. Drinks less alcohol, moderate sexual drive.

8.7 Gifts of The Holy Spirit

The gifts of the Holy Spirit completes and perfect the virtues by helping those who receive them respond more to the prompting of the Holy Spirit, again those who possess sanctifying grace are able to act according to the FRUITS OF THE HOLY SPIRIT: charity, joy, peace, patience, kindness, goodness, generosity, gentleness, faithfulness, modesty chastity and self-control.

Those who possess sanctifying grace perform the Spiritual and Corporal Work of Mercy

A. Corporal work of Mercy.
1. Feed the hungry
2. Giving drink to the thirsty
3. Sheltering the homeless
3. Clothing the naked
4. Visiting the sick
5. Visiting the imprisoned
6. Bury the dead

B. The Spiritual works of Mercy.
1. Admonishing the sinner
2. Instructing the ignorant
3. Counseling the doubtful
4. Comforting the sorrowful
5. Bearing wrongs patiently.

How do we receive or obtain the sanctifying grace, The Lord gave this to us through our baptismal promises with the grace of justification which enables us to believe in one God (TRINITY) to hope in Him, to Love Him with all our hearts. God seals His people, so that believers have that confidence.

Our salvation is secured by His Holy Spirit on the day of the "Pentecost". Believe and see what the Lord has done, the 144,000 Jewish believers received their seals on the day of" Peter's first sermon"; the apostle received theirs on the day of "Pentecost" and the people who came for "Revival and Retreat" the day following the Pentecost, received same gifts as well, One God .(God the Father, God the Son and The Holy Spirit). And since then all around the world it has happened ever since, Christianity the followers of Jesus.

8.8 Faith what is it? (ESV, HEBREW. 1.1-39)

V1" Faith is the assurance of things hoped for and the conviction of things not seen". We all have false sense of security either we want to accept it or not but is always there, sometimes we hold dearly to things we shouldn't, cause undue stress to self and soul. Those people who are sick in the hospital, if you asked them, they will rather be somewhere else than being in the hospital with a nurse or an hospital minister at bedside, most of us are running on empty, our spiritual tank is empty, when someone tells you to pick-up your cross and walk with Jesus, it meant we must pick-up our cross and follow Jesus, because there is no any other name given that we can be saved. Here are some problems many patients who access the healthcare and I admitted for hospital stay are going through: They expressed during initial interview as an admission nurse.

1. Fear of unknown
2. Fear of hopelessness
3. Lack of faith: some left the spiritual care side of admission document blank/or skip it
4. Fear of helplessness
5. Fear of abandonment by families
6. Fear of financial instability

7. Fear of death

Today if you're sick from that million dollars job you think you have, will someone from your job visited you, do you think in about a month after gone for so long, the company will keep the job for you, so how vulnerable are you now, the point Iam making is to get us start talking about things that make us vulnerable or that will give us an idea to plan and not put all our eggs in one basket as total depending on another person or information, we should try and find thing out for ourselves.

The only person that has our interest at heart is Jesus Christ who came from Heaven to rescue us from chain of poverty, helplessness, hopelessness and the unknowns.

He told us to in the process of us making money and building our portfolio we should put our own needs first and foremost and trust Him, yes seek the money but don't allow it to dominate you and your entire existence. Remember the gambler song, Kenny Roger song know when to fold up and walk away? we should also be smart, we can have wealth but what good is the wealth when there is no value or integrated –principle to benefit others, then we become those fictional characters we read about in some novels.

I sincerely hope we live the life God Almighty has mapped out for us, the lives that we take us to His beautiful Home in Heaven. Here is (NIV, Matthew. 6.33). "But seek ye first the kingdom of God and His righteousness and all these things shall be added unto you" Jesus instructs us to prioritize our Eternal salvation and make gaining entry to Heaven a matter of urgency, we should not leave it to chance, we can't delegate the work involve with it, we must earn it and be proud of working for Jesus in our brothers and sisters. Another passage to remind us the work of our Lord will be (NASB, Matthew. 16.24-28). The more we know, whoever loses his life for My sake will find it. 26 For what will it profit a man if he gains the whole world and forfeits his soul? Or what will a man give in exchange for his soul? 27 For the Son of Man is going to come in the glory of His Father with His angels and will then repay every man according to his deeds.

28 "Truly I say to you, there are some of those who are standing here who will not taste death until they see the Son of Man coming in His kingdom."

We have moved now from our comfort zone-meaning we are now in a healthcare setting, this journey is solely individualized, and as your nurse plan your care, for those you declared their spirituality in the area of denomination in case of spiritual distress while navigating and accessing care, we have to start from self, how many information should we as patient withhold for those who takes care of us, our spirituality, our faith or who we believe at that point should have been settle, for example at age 50 plus, some still struggle with faith and some refused to take advantage of what the hospitals have to offer and suffer silently in a modern time, some still can't talk honestly without offending some people about their faith candidly, and I asked myself "Why" what and how is this happening, when you explored the reasons they gave you, not in a judgmental way but for rationality sake, you come to the conclusion that they were never told by those who raised them, nor were they assisted at the home they grew up, some homes find it hard to talk about their faith, whether you're a Christian, or others. So, when these people grew-up, they still wouldn't talk about it because there are no experiences to draw from.

God is real, He came to save us from our sins, and for those who repent and believe in Jesus-they are save and become children of God. Some of the patients visited requested baptism before the y leave the hospital, some requested communion after so many years, after their reconciliation and penance, this cut through denomination boundary, we have to remain relevant in our faith and have a little perspective about it, there is difference between religion and faith, but both are mutually inclusive.

"34 But when the Pharisees heard that Jesus had silenced the Sadducees, they gathered themselves together. 35 One of them,]a lawyer, asked Him a question, testing Him, 36 "Teacher, which is the great commandment in the Law?" 37 And He said to him, "'You shall love the Lord your God with all your heart, and with all your soul, and with all your mind.' 38 This is the great and]foremost commandment. 39 The second is like it, 'You shall love your neighbor as yourself.' 40 On these two commandments depend the whole Law and the Prophets." (NASB, Matthew. 22.34-40,).

During our journey of faith, we picked up some added bags, which we should not have carried we left the path and we tried   to do things our ways, so the journey instead of some pleasantry, weighted us down and it becomes a burden, unpleasant encounter, examples of these forces within us are: Envy, Jealousy, Rage, Impatience.

The point Iam making is that we can change that. By following Jesus and repent of our sins, we can reconnect and join Our Lord for service to other, we can start using those talents to shape and work for God glory. Jesus said in (ESV, Matthew. 11.28). "Come to me, all ye that labor and are heavy laden, and I will give you rest. So, we must all come to Jesus, repent of our sins, and become children of God once again.

Yes, we came from different regions of this great planet, East, West, South and North. Our nationalities are our strength. When someone is sick, alone in the hospital by themselves, no visitors, families already gone for the day's work, you 're staring at the ceiling in your room and contemplating how your day or lives will turn out, the only thing left for that individual which nobody can take away is yourself and your God" you meditate and said, Lord I know you can hear me, I need your help today.

Then for once in our individual life, the soul recognizes its own limitations. God is always around He got His eyes on the universal. As I shared my work log and visiting log even though I start late in life, and the gift of sharing, life, we all will agree, with God time is endless. We put limit to how or how far our Lord should go with us, without us knowing it. I hope you can find yourself in the story of our God-Holy Trinity, regardless of your social, economic and racial background, we are all in one big family as Christians, brothers and sisters in Christ.

CHAPTER 9:
Spirituality Awakening and Aging

With advancing age, sickness or crisis may lead to a rethinking, a re-evaluation of one's life and what has guided a person religiously or spiritually?

Spirituality.

1. The quality of being concerned with the human spirit or soul as opposed to material or physical things.

The shift in priorities allows us to embrace our spirituality in a more profound way "The pastoral care of the sick" is the focus of this project. The gospel of Jesus Christ is yet moving again to God's people direction, wherever they go Jesus is in their midst. Jesus told the first Apostle Peter, in (ESV, Matthew. 4.18-22). Jesus Calls the First Disciples18 While walking by the Sea of Galilee, he saw two brothers, Simon (who is called Peter) and Andrew his brother, casting a net into the sea, for they were fishermen. 19 And he said to them, "Follow me, and I will make you fishers of men."[a] 20 Immediately they left their nets and followed Jesus.

The aging process, the experience of moving into and through different developmental phases affects the spirit and therefore one's spiritual life. (Brower 2006).

"Spirit" derived from the Latin spiritus, meaning "soul, courage, vigor, breath" our spirit is our vital center or our core. And the "spiritual" are those things which support that center which gives us a sense of courage, or heart, for our living.

Spiritual experiences are those events in life and moments in relationships which connect us to that vital or animating force within and which give greater meaning and depth to our day-to-day living.

Add to that, when grace is operating in our souls, it doesn't just mean that God is helping us to do certain things or to live certain ways. It actually means that God is doing these things Himself and that He is inviting us in the process. In other words, when grace is present in us, we are no longer the ones who are primarily doing the work. (Destefano 130).

Naturally, that which moves the spirit that which brings us deep meaning and satisfaction and piloting us at 45 years of age may not be what nurtures our sense of wholeness and spiritual wellness at 80 or 90. So, in my view, the process of aging at every life stage brings about changes in one's spiritual life.

Some of the events within the latter stages of life which may prompt spiritual growth, or an overhaul of the religious life are well documented and commonly experienced by us as individuals. Successful aging requires self-esteem which is the foundation of psychosocial health and spirituality. (Christensen & Cockcrow 1590). Being value by others and treated with respect builds self-esteem.

Nurses have roles as advocate to dispel the myths associated with aging and to educate people to the realities of aging and options that are available. During admission process, nurses gathered information from psychosocial to medical problems and finally we arrive to nurse diagnoses with care plan and action/intervention, each patient care is individualized, just like their spiritual care is also individualized.

We allow the patient to take ownership of their spiritual aspect and guide the nurses how to move forward, just because you as an individual check Methodist or catholic or Lutheran on the admission box, does not give me the nurse permission to solicit any faith randomly coming to your room at any time, you must still give us the permission to allow them to come to your room in the hospital, just as you will inform us to get or call the spiritual care department for you on your behalf.

Once you're in hospital, other processes take over, you no longer in your Zone, we cater to make your experience in the hospital a pleasant one, but you have to let us know how far we can go. The primary goal in your care plan is to get you out of the bed as soon as possible to rejoin your family and your life.

Some adults when they get to hospital during illness the coping mechanism is not really there, some during interview thought this illnesses right now is their fault, instead of managing it the right way, and some families members are enablers, rather than helping the adults to cope with illnesses, they add their own problems with it, thereby either prolonging the stay or the adults gave up completely and there are sets back.

We need to respect people and allow them to make decision for themselves. The Maslow is about our human needs but transfer over to a broader picture in human condition which affects any human beings depending on what is going on with that particular person at the time.

Maslow hierarchy of needs is self-worth measurement on individuals which includes spiritual aspect of self. For some people, this is a major factor. We can run but we can't hide, this could be potentially complicated if we ignore who we really are.

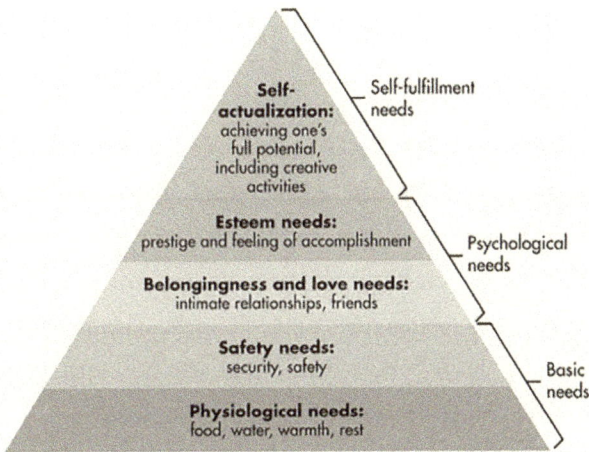

Figure 3

9.1 Self-Appraisal

Remininiscence and Life Review, this is story period for older adults, some events for them are positive and adaptive, other events are not when they have to do the appraisal how much their lives are worth with monetary value. Most older adult attached greater value to religious beliefs and behavior.(Berk 591). See figure 3 below with explanation how people measure themselves in relation to lifetime achievement and worth.

Maslow allows us to take inner picture and do examination of self, which is our conscience, to see whether indeed we are worth what we project, ourselves to be or we were just faking it all this time (see figure.3). For those who care so much for the earthly materialistic things, as you get old, it will start making sense that the good we paid so much for are indeed worthless, when you are sick and nobody at the end of that door to visit you, you will remember what Jesus has been telling you from beginning of time, do not lay treasure up in here, but seek the things from above. Ask yourself this question, Heaven can wait; Can Heaven wait? No, Jesus already decreed it, we must go through it like He did at the appointed time, so we must equip ourselves.

Jesus said in (NASB, John. 14. 1-6,). 14 "Do not let your heart be troubled; believe in God, believe also in Me. 2 In My Father's house are many dwelling places; if it were not so, I would have told you; for I go to prepare a place for you. 3 If I go and prepare a place for you, I will come again and receive you to Myself, that where I am, there you may be also. 4 And you know the way where I am going." 5 Thomas *said to Him, "Lord, we do not know where You are going, how do we know the way?" 6 Jesus *said to him, "I am the way, and the truth, and the life; no one comes to the Father but through Me",

"Be anxious for nothing, but in everything by prayer and supplication, with thanksgiving, let your requests be made known to

God; and the peace of God, which surpasses all understanding, will guard your hearts and minds through Christ Jesus. Amen (Philippians 4:6-7 NASB).

Jesus said yet another promise "Abide in me, and I in you, As the branch cannot bear fruit of itself, unless it abides in the vine, neither can you, unless you abide in me. Iam the vine, you are the branches. He who abides in Me, and I in Him, bears much fruit; for without Me you can do nothing. "If anyone does not abide in Me, he is cast out as a branch and is withered; and they gather them and throw them into the fire, and they are burned. If you abide in Me, and my Words abide in you, you will ask what you desire, and it shall be done for you". (NIV, John 15.4-7).

We are explorers, sharing ideas with each other to make this universe a better universe, but now, we are afraid of each other. Which is why portion of this persuasive project will be devoted to talk about "Cultural Diversity" and how it relates to our spirituality.

Healthcare is changing and Christianity is changing with it, gone are the days, when someone get sick and had to wait forever for his/ her pastor to come visit, or for that matter the members congregation, most hospitals now not just in USA, but around the world are stepping up to the plate to bring spirituality to their patients as part of added benefit when admitted in the hospital, all that patient had to do is declare church affiliation upon arrival, and the spiritual care department is automatically consulted for the entire duration or stay for that individual patients, we are moving up, and these churches must buckle up and follow the trending. Where the churches lack, hospital pick up the tabs.

9.2 Cultural Diversity Hospital Ministry.

Understanding diversity? It is understanding the differences that make each person unique, understanding them and appreciating the differences we bring help

1. Individual persons: Those who gain new insights, while enjoying new relationships

2. Communities-The processes that can tap those various talents of their members to help meet our individual person's goal and group goals.

3. Groups: These come about through classroom, corporations. When our uniqueness is respected, productivity improve, businesses that appreciate diversity have leading edge and advantage over status-quo entity in today global market place.

9.3 What Make Each Person Unique? (ESV, Luke 12. 4-7)

"I tell you, my friends, do not fear those who kill the body, and after that have nothing more that they can do. "But I warn you whom to fear, fear Him who, after has killed, has authority to cast into hell. "Yes, I tell you, fear Him. Are not five sparrows sold for two pennies? And not one of them is forgotten before God. "Why, even the hairs of your head are all numbered.

Fear not, you are of more value than many sparrows". In our own estimation, there are many things that make us special and unique, for examples, Appearance, gender, family, age, sexual orientation, income and social status, religious, spiritual, our philosophical beliefs, life experiences and educational background. Understanding diversity begins from within, how we view ourselves and our world and each other in the universe with us.

When we judge other people before getting to know them, we have just miss an opportunity to connect with another person in this journey both of us are trekking, we lose that chance to hear or share what information our Lord wanted them to share at that particular moment, and we will never hear them again, because, our Lord Manages our Time, He is the keeper of every body's time on Earth, whether we debate or not, He had already reconciled with our Heavenly Father the precise moment, from conception to our natural death nobody can change it, we must as well just pay attention and hear each other out, we should not assume anything,

We should be open minded to things to get clarity on idea, we should encourage questions to get answers, and we develop friendships with people of different background. Jesus will ask us how we treat one another. God's presence in our lives as a matter of fact produces peace within us, people we encounter in our day-to-day interaction matter.

The relationship with God produces purpose driven talented encounter, and dynamite power surge the path of resolute and impact people along the path we go through. God given purpose in our lives provides understanding which allows us to be all that God's wants us to accomplish. We must avoid prejudice and stereotypes one another because the behavior hurts everyone, and we offend God when we do that, this attitude limit our opportunities with each other, also it makes the person being rejected to feel little and we devalue God's creation which we are. We have to pray that whatever our Lord calls us for, may we not go back to Him empty handed. Amen.

9.4 The Weapon of Spiritual Warfare
(ESV, Ephesians 6.10-20)

Fifth in our series of reasons to pray is that prayer is a major weapon in fighting the spiritual battle. Ephesians six, verses ten to twenty, outlines some of many ways to pray to God. We are reminded that ultimately our struggles are not against humans, but against powerful spiritual beings and forces in the "heavenly places" (the spiritual realm which directly influences the natural, material realm).

The picture here is that of a war. Life as a Christian is not a playground; it's a battlefield. While there is much beauty and love in the world, it is often bent and twisted by our fall and Satan's machinations. Thus, the war for souls between God and Satan is fought with Christian co-combatants with Him.

We are instructed by Paul, an experienced soldier in this combat, to be appropriately clad and armed for our struggle. In this passage, he uses some of the most vivid imagery in the New Testament. Modeling a Roman Legionnaire, we put on the helmet of salvation, the breastplate of righteousness, loins girded with truth, feet shod with the preparation of the Gospel, shield of faith, sword of the Spirit (the Word of God).

The weapon of prayer softens up Satan's fortress. Hell's gates cannot prevail. It is the cannon, reducing the wall to rubble so that the troops can go through. Too often, the gospel moves slowly because the softening-up process of prayer has been neglected. When practiced, however, prayer "puts the wind at the back" of Christ's soldiers.

Apostle Paul is not playing here, you struggle with your faith, you attend all those classes why you should renounce the devil and follow Christ, you finally got your break through and you think that's it.

No, the battle just starts, the devil knows you're Jesus child and will do anything to upset that, so stay with Jesus now to reveal the plan of the enemies to you, because the Sanctifying grace you obtain during your baptismal oath will now come to play on your behalf, you will be able to add two and two together equal 4 and not 3 or 2 and see that there are evil in the world, pay attention to yourself and others. You have joined your hands with God now to fight the rebels; this means none of your needs will go unsupplied alleluia. God is rich enough to grant us what we need in our daily struggles, we must each day come to the Throne of Grace with confidence, boldly with humility, confessed the sins if they make you come short, and let past go. Look at these Bible passages: (psalm 66:18), I John 1:9; and John 21-22;

and Roman 8:1; all these Bible passage should help to provide comfort and guidance.

9.5 Our Invisible Friends; Angel in Our Midst

There are many different depictions of angels in the world today. We are fascinated by the idea of heavenly beings and it's not hard to find jewelry, art, or even garden decorations with tiny baby cherub or elegant beings. In the book entitled Angels, Billy Graham told the story of Dr. Mitchell, w well known doctor, who was awakened from sleep one rainy night by a little girl, poorly dressed and very upset, she said her mother was very sick, and wanted the doctor to come right away and treat her. Doctor went treated the patient but found out she has no daughter and that she died three weeks earlier.

NIV, Luke. 20.35). "But those who are considered worthy of taking part in the age to come and in the resurrection from the dead will neither marry nor be given in marriage, 36 and they can no longer die; for they are like the angels. They are God's children, since they are children of the resurrection.

30 At the resurrection people will neither marry nor be given in marriage; they will be like the angels in heaven. This was a respond by Jesus for those who wanted to know how to get themselves ready for Heaven. (NIV, Matthew. 22.30). The angel Gabriel visited Mary in (NIV, Luke. 1. 26-30).

26 Six months after Elizabeth had become pregnant, God sent the angel Gabriel to Nazareth, a city in Galilee. 27 The angel went to a virgin promised in marriage to a descendant of David named Joseph. The virgin's name was Mary.

28 When the angel entered her home, he greeted her and said, "You are favored by the Lord! The Lord is with you."

29 She was startled by what the angel said and tried to figure out what

this greeting meant. Many scholars have shared in their experiences how Angels revealed what Heaven and Earth would be like. A man was revealed the secrets chambers of St. Michael and got to tour it while writing the messages down on a handkerchief, the nine choirs, it became St. Michael Prayer. We are not alone, angels are in our midst. Again angel Raphael revealed his identity in (NASB, Tobit. 12. 1-22). V15 "Iam Raphael, one of the seven angels who stand and serve before the Glory of the Lord." So, our lives have never been a waste of God's time nor ours either, we must try and ask Him to journey with us.

Our Lord will not leave us here without some kind of protection, throughout Old Testament; they're very frequent visitors... Our world is so noisy now that the only time they get our attention is during sleep, or we receive a vision any time. Sometimes we count our Lord's out in our daily activities, we often forget, He's the owner of the universe, He owns both the physical realms and spiritual realms, but Loved us so much and gave us space to explore our talents and our lives due to the free will nature we acquired from Him.

The three principal angels we know without giving or assuming their names are, Michael, Gabriel and St. Raphael. God's angels are all around us, to guide, to encourage, to protect, they serve as a ministering Spirit, when we made mistake to help us not to make the same mistake again. Without going to much details, since ¾ of population believe they existed before us or God allowed them to be just as He was creating us. The visit of Mary and her cousin Elizabeth by two Angel were fully documented in the sacred scripture. God created them to work for Him.

9.6 Questions and Answers About the Angels

1. What is an angel? An angel is a spirit that is a creature who does

not have a body

2. Angels are real person because they have mind and will.

3. How do you know there are angels the Bible mentions them about 300 hundred time?

4. Does everyone have a guardian angel? Yes, God appoints an angel to watch over every human. "See that you despise not one of these little ones, for I say to you, that their angels in Heaven always see the face of my Father who is in Heaven. (NIV, Matthew. 18.10).

5. We read and told that they have spectacular powers that are cosmic in magnitude.

6. Prodigious which means they have armies, legions and multitudes

7. They have "system of ranking" they live in a society.

8. Christianity teaches that the primary thing that distinguishes angels from the rest of creature is that they are "pure Spirits"

So due to being pure Spirit no restrictions, they 're not bound by constant of physical space. So, angels of our Lord are extraordinary creatures.

"The intellect of an angel is incomparably superior to the human intellect

The human mind has to plot from truth, just as the human body moves step by step, whereas

The angelic intelligence   grasps the whole of a subject at a single glance. They have supernatural knowledge. (O'Sullivan Paul).

9. Did all the Angels obey God?

No, some of them, led by Lucifer, or Satan, disobeyed God and were sent immediately in to hell. These are the fallen angels or devils.

"And there was a great battle in Heaven, Michael and his angel fought with the dragon, and the dragon fought and his angels. And they prevailed not, neither was their place found any more in heaven." They were sent to hell. (NIV, Revelation. 12.7-8).

9.7 A Poem by Lucy Jo

A Dedication to My Guardian Angel
It's a fact well known, Since the day I was born
I need not fear.
Your presence is always near.
When God assigned you to me
He knew what a challenge I would be
You came to be my guardian light
The goodness in me is due to your insight
Your speacialty is me
How lucky can I be
Iam so grateful, for your friendship and your love,
Which sometimes comes in the form of a dove
You bless me with your strength and courage
I strive to conform to your holy image.
When I'm distressed and in need, you plant a seed,
And nurture me to grow in grace and wisdom
So I will be worthy to enter our Lord's Kingdom
Your gentle breeze reminds me,
Since the older I get, lest I forget
To thank you for being my best friend
Stay with me, My very own angel
Until the end
When in Heaven we will meet again.

9.8 Summary Failure to Finish Move and See

People get tired and lost, and therefore do not go fast or far enough. To achieve success requires ability to focus and refocus for the task at hand. God is merciful. (NIV, Ezekiel. 33.11). Jesus said, "I take no pleasure in the death of the wicked man, says the Lord, but rather in his conversion that he may live". And the second passage of saving grace of our Lord could be found in (ESV, John. 11.25-26). "I'm the resurrection and the Life says the Lord, whoever believe in me, even if he dies, will live"

If someone tells you not to worry about Heaven and Hell, please take the matter into your hand and go and read about it, for this last assignment nobody should delegate it to any person, because it is individualized. We should care about God's home, He said "Iam going home to prepare a place for you, where Iam you will be also". His kingdom is not of this world, so Heaven cannot wait, this too we must pass through it.

Jesus said, "My sheep hear my voice. I know them, and they follow me. I give them eternal life, and they shall never perish. No one can take them out of my hand. My father, who has given them to me, is greater than all, and no one can take them out of the Father's hand. The Father and I are one. (NIV, John. 10.27-30). Jesus laid down His life for His sheep and willingly died for them, and by the third day, He rose from the dead. Jesus death on the cross was real, there was no dress rehearsal. It was a permanent encounter. He dies for us and warned every one of us to follow Him. The beatitudes of Jesus Christ should make everyone happy that if we follow Him, our lives here on earth will mimic that of His Heavenly Kingdom, and here is the reminder of what Jesus said in Beatitudes. (NIV, Matthew. 5.3-10).

3 "Blessed are the poor in spirit, for theirs is the kingdom of heaven.

4 Blessed are those who mourn, for they will be comforted.

5 Blessed are the meek, for they will inherit the earth.

6 Blessed are those who hunger and thirst for righteousness, for they will be filled.

7 Blessed are the merciful, for they will be shown mercy.

8 Blessed are the pure in heart, for they will see God.

9 Blessed are the peacemakers, for they will be called children

of God.

10 Blessed are those who are persecuted because of righteousness, for theirs is the kingdom of heaven.

In the above passage Jesus promises us happiness. In fact, the word "blessed" means "happy." The Beatitudes are at the core of Christ's teaching. They fulfill the promise made to the Jewish people by pointing beyond earthly happiness to the eternal happiness of heaven. The reward promised in each of the Beatitudes is primarily heaven. If we live according to His Divine plan for our lives, as Children of God we would have foretaste of the happiness of Heaven in this world of ours.

One Saint that stood out in this discovery of faith was Saint Therese of Lisieux. Regardless of your church affiliates as Christians, we should not deny anybody the grace of our Lord, when life's events seems complicated or unreachable, her simple nature with humor in the" story of a soul" will inspire anybody. She told God during her prayer that, Lord I don't know what to do because there were lots of notable people before me and Iam just a little flower in your Garden, please help me to do my best to serve you in my own little way. The same goes to every one of us, with humility and caring heart our Lord will help us to be all we can be in this world. If we only be ourselves. Jesus taught us the act of humility, charity with brotherly and sisterly love.

Jesus. Himself came down from Heaven and takes our human nature because of the Love He had for mankind. All of beatitudes have an eschatological meaning with promise of salvation, not in this world but in Heaven, but if we follow our Lord Jesus Christ teachings and persevere in our faith, we could live and enjoy this world like we're in Heaven already, let Jesus lead us because the opposite of beatitudes is misery.

Let us share a letter from St. Paul to the Romans here and put our life journey in a clear perspective. (NIV, Romans. 14.7-9). "Brothers and sisters; none of us lives for oneself, and no one dies for oneself. For if we live, we live for the Lord, and if we die, we die for the Lord; so then, whether we live or die, we are the Lord's. For this is why Christ died and came to life, that He might be the Lord of both the dead and the living".

I hope I have persuaded you to at least check the four-last judgement of our Lord and be empowered. From the beginning of my project to the end of this writing, I sincerely hope you found yourself in the story of our God. His story is our story, and our story is His. May the good Lord perfect everything that concerns each and every one of us, and May we be blessed and witness His resurrection in His Kingdom and be counted with His Holy Angels. Amen

In closing I would like to share a poem with my audiences written by Lucy Jo, and a Bible passage about freedom of choice in (NRSV, Sirach.15.15-20).

15 If you choose, you can keep the commandments,
    and to act faithfully is a matter of your own choice.

16 He has placed before you fire and water;
    stretch out your hand for whichever you choose.

17 Before each person are life and death,
    and whichever one chooses will be given.

18 For great is the wisdom of the Lord;
    he is mighty in power and sees everything;

19 his eyes are on those who fear him,
    and he knows every human action.

20 He has not commanded anyone to be wicked,
    and He has not given anyone permission to sin.

9.9 Sermon on the Mount and Crossroad
(English Standard Version. Mathew 5. 1-16).

What a perfect Landscape. In V-1 Our Lord went up on the mountain, and then He sat down with His disciples and others again, to deliver the most sophisticated and powerful preaching of a lifetime. The setting was spectacular on top of a mountain overlooking sea of Galilee. For this discussion, "What's at Stake? Eternity of course.

I will use the invitation Method for the discussion, and this is found on page 20 under meditation guide number 7. Readers are encouraged and invited to share by names with freedom to pass, and if you are journaling alone, please at the end share your thoughts later with a friend. Sermon on the mount was and is about Love Jesus has for us. The sermon's about the way of life, the expansion of the golden rule- holy ways—meaning do unto others as you want to be done unto you. It reminded us the commandments of God in Jesus gentle ways. If we (His people) Love Him so much, we must do the beatitudes. Then comes the question of crossroad in our lives.

By definition (Merriam-Webster, 1828), stated it's a point at which a crucial decision must be made that will have far-reaching consequences. As Christians we cannot let our guard down, we must pray always for God guidance and protection in our journey of faith, we must proceed with caution looking both ways on entering any given intersection in our lives. May the good Lord continue to perfect all our imperfections, help us to grow in all the necessary virtues, His seven gifts of the Holy Spirit, and the twelve fruits of the holy spirit as Jesus eloquently preached in His Sermon on the mount. We pray Lord, for Hope, Faith, Charity and to Love our God as we carry our own cross to follow His footsteps. Amen.

CHAPTER 10:
Conclusion

10.0 Conclusion For Us By Lucy Jo

Two thousand years ago,
God sent His only begotten son, so His will could be done.
He stayed for just a little while,
But for us, He went a mile.
He came, the wonder of it all,
And is available when we call
He provides for all our needs,
As we follow where He leads.
He taught us to "about face"
In adversity, keep our place.
He tells us to love one another
And to have faith and hope,
Virtues we need to cope
For us, Jesus sacrificed His Life
Oh, at what a price!
For us, He conquered evil and strife.
Believers will inherit eternal Life
God holds the world in His hands,
And sometimes we don't understand.
We know what is best for us, when we put our trust in Jesus
By uniting with Him, we become one body, one soul,
His will is our goal, every word He gave us,
We hold dear and are like music to our ears.
We praise you, our savior supreme,
Our glorious, omnipotent King

Because you came for us,
Our beloved Jesus.

Finally, I end the book with Ten Songs from good old Christians hymnal book.1). African American Heritage Hymnal, 2). OCP and 3). GIA Publications. For those who will use this book for retreat, revival and Bible study in US/ globally. Email or write me at the address provided at the back of the book, a copy of the songs will be mail to you-free. E mail Salvereginainternationals@gmail.com and Postal address: P. O. Box 1515, Bellaire, Texas 77402

Thank you, Agnes.

1. Lord of the Dance
2. Lead me Lord
3. Sing a New Song
4. The Glory of These forty Days
5. What A Friend We Have In Jesus
6. I am Redeemed
7. Whatsoever You Do
8. I am The Bread Of Life
9. Here I am Lord
10. I have decided to follow Jesus

Bibliography

1. Anders, Max. *30 days to Understand the Bible. Nashville, Tennessee. Thomas Nelson Literary Agency Wolgemuth and Associates 2011*

2. Alz.org/end-of-life-decision. web. 1 Sep. 2016

3. Black, Stewart., and Gregersen, Hal. *It Starts with One. Pulling It All Together. Upper Saddle River, New Jersey. Pearson Education and Wharton School Publishing. 2002.*

4. Batterson, Mark. *Praying Circles Around Your Children. Austin, Texas. Fedd and Company, 2012*

5. Berk, Laura. *Development Through the Lifespan. Needham Heights, Massachusetts.*

6. Brower, J. *Faith, Spirituality and Awakening. Frontline why. 23 Apr 2006. web. 18 Aug 2017.*

7. Communication theory.org/Maslow's-hierarchy-of-needs/. web 20 Aug 2017

8. Douay-Rheims 1899 American Edition (DRA

9. Christensen, Barbara., and Kockrow, Elaine. *Foundations of Nursing 2nd edition. St. Louis, Missouri. Mosby 1995*

10. Canary, John. *Worship. Chicago, Illinois. GIA Publications, Inc. 4th edition 2011*

11. CrefloDollarMinistries.org date 9 Nov 2016 web. 26 June 2017

12. Davies, Paul. *The Mind of God. New York, New York. Simon and Schuster Paperbacks. 1992.*

13. Destefano, Anthony. *Angels All Around Us. New York. New York. Doubleday Religion Crown Publishing. 2011*

14. English Standard Version. *Bible Gateway. Web. 25 Oct. 2016*

15. Francis, Collins. *The Language of God. New York, New York. Simon and Schuster, Inc. 2006.*

16. Flynn, Vinny. *Seven Secrets of Confession. Stockbridge, Massachusetts. Mercy Song Ignatius Press. 2013.*

17. Geisler, Norman. *Chosen but Free. Bloomington, Minnesota. Bethany House Publisher, 2010*

18. Harris, Maria. *The Seven Steps of Women Spirituality. New York, New York. Bantan Doubleday Dell Publishing Groups, Inc.1989.*

19. Kratz, Lucy. *A dedication to my Guardian A dedication to my Guardian Angel. Best Poems Compilation. Personal Interview. 18 Sep. 2015. Houston Texas.*

20. Krattz, Lucy. *For us." Best Poems Compilation." Personal interview. 18 Sep. 2015.Houston, Texas*

21. Lee, Albert." Storm Of Life" NP. http://odb.org/2015/10/30/the-storm-of-life. web. 26 Aug,2017

22. Martin, James. My Life with Saints. Chicago, Illinois. Loyola Press. 2007

23. Merton, Thomas. The Seven Storey Mountain. New York, New York. Houghton Mifflin Harcourt Publishing Company. 1999.

24. Rhodes, Ron. 40 Days Through Revelation. Eugene, Oregon. Harvest House Publishers. 2013.

25. English Standard Version Bible. Wheaton, Illinois Crossway Publishing Ministry of Good News Publishers, 2007. Print.

26. http://www.Merriam-Webster.com/dictionary/ecumenical web. 26 July. 2017.

27. http://gerontologist.oxfordjournal.org/content/42/suppl_3/24. Print. 2016.

28. Holy Bible, New International Version Colorado Springs, Colorado. Biblica Inc., 1984.

29. New American Standard Bible. New York, New York. Oxford University Press. 2006. Print.

30. New King James Version. Nashville, Tennessee. Thomas Nelson.1994. Print

31. New Revised Standard Version 1989 the Division of Christian Education of the National Council of the Churches of Christ in the United States of America.

32. http://www.prayers-for-special-help.com/bible-verse-about-heaven.html. web. 18 July 2014.

33. http//ww.pewresearch.org/fact-tant/2017/04/05christains-remains-world-largest-religions-group-but-they-are-declining-in-europe/ web. 1 Sep. 2017.

34. Purdue Owl. "MLA Formatting and Style Guide". Web 18 July 2017 https://owl.english.purdue.edu/owl/owlprint/747/

35. http://www.whatchristainswanttoknow.com web. 24 Nov 2016.

36. www.OLRL.org/The Reality of Hell. web. 13 May. 2016.

37. https://biblegateway.com/versins/english-standard-version-esv-bible/ Web 24 Aug 2017

38. https://stjosemaria.org/I [ray-sermon-on-the-mount. Web 24 Aug 2017

www.ingramcontent.com/pod-product-compliance
Lightning Source LLC
Chambersburg PA
CBHW020453100426
42813CB00031B/3350/J